Keyboarding

Keyboarding

Derek Stananought, BEd(Hons), FRSA, has many years of involvement with keyboarding on all types of equipment including telex, word processors, computers, and typewriters (manual, electric and electronic). He was formerly Senior Lecturer at Manchester Polytechnic.

Derek has been involved as an examiner for word processing and other subjects for several years. He is well known as a writer and lecturer in this country and overseas and more recently has become involved with the production of teaching and learning materials concerned with information processing.

Keyboarding

A Universal Approach to Basic Typewriting Skills

Derek Stananought

Consultant Editor: Joyce Stananought

Chambers Commerce Series

© Derek Stananought 1987

Published by W & R Chambers Ltd Edinburgh, 1987

British Library Cataloguing in Publication Data

Stananought, Derek
   Keyboarding.—(Chambers commerce series)
   1. Word processing   2. Electronic data
   processing—Keyboarding
   I.Title
   652'.5   Z52.4

ISBN 0-550-20705-8 /12

Typeset by Waddie & Co. Ltd Edinburgh

Printed in Great Britain by
Richard Clay Ltd, Bungay, Suffolk

Contents

Chapter 33   File Copies

Chapter 34   Setting Information Out in Table Form

Chapter 35   Decimal Alignment and Right Alignment of Columns

Chapter 36   Review and Revision

Answers

Preface

The aim of this book is to provide a unified approach to the acquisition of keyboarding skills. It deals with manual typewriters, electric and electronic typewriters, dedicated word processors (computers designed specifically for typewriting) and computers. The wealth of background information provided on the new technology area makes it ideal for the open learning approach. The book is written as a self-teach package, but is equally applicable for use under the guidance of a teacher. It will also prove useful for proficient typists who wish to transfer their keyboarding skills to the alternative requirements of word processors and computers.

The book deals with the knowledge required before a learner begins to type; guidelines on how to type; tips; background information associated with the new technology; exercises, along with instructions; methods of enhancing the appearance of typed documents; and review and revision material.

Five types of exercise are included: keyboarding, proof-reading, speed development, practical application of typing skills, and revision. The proof-reading exercises can be used as additional practice material once the keyboard has been mastered. The speed development exercises are intended to help you increase your typing speed. They may also be used to measure your typewriting speed.

For the purpose of this book the word *computer* is used as an 'umbrella term' for either a computer running a word processing package or a dedicated word processor.

In office terms the word *typist* is used to describe a person who sits at a typewriter and types, and the word *operator* to describe a person who sits at a computer and inputs information. The word *typist* only is used throughout this book for the purpose of continuity of expression.

D. S.

Introduction

1.1 How to Use This Book

It is hoped that you will read the whole of this book and thereby widen your knowledge of keyboarding. You are likely to find manual typewriters, electric and electronic typewriters, word processors and computers all in one office nowadays. Consequently, it would be beneficial to have an overall knowledge of keyboarding for all these machines if you intend to work in an office. However it is recognised that some people may wish to concentrate on one particular area only, and to this end chapters 1-7 are designed in such a way that you may select those parts most applicable to your needs. *Icons* (small drawings to represent the different equipment) are used to highlight information associated with the various machines, as follows:

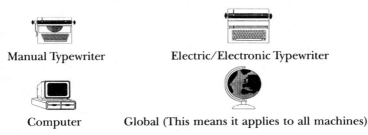

Manual Typewriter	Electric/Electronic Typewriter
Computer	Global (This means it applies to all machines)

The following additional icons are used in other chapters:

Proofreading	What Does It Mean?

You may progress through the first part of the book by looking for the icon appropriate to your machine. In addition all learners are advised to read the *Global* areas. The exercises are applicable to all machines and you are advised to progress through them in sequence. It will be beneficial to you to read the whole of each chapter before starting to type the associated exercise(s).

1.2 What Is a Keyboard?

A keyboard is any board or base on which there are keys. A key is pressed to cause something to happen. With a typewriter a letter is printed on paper.

At first, keyboards were an integral part of a typewriter, but the types of keyboard available have changed considerably in recent years. Various forms of keyboard are to be found in today's offices and homes on typewriters, computers, and calculators. When we learn how to use these keyboards, we are learning keyboarding skills. Keyboards are often separate units, connected to the computer—or typewriter—by means of a cable.

1.3 Why Use a Keyboard?

People use keyboards for various reasons. Some wish to follow a career in which typewriting skills are esssential—secretary, journalist, typesetter, etc. Managers find that the company they work for records all business data on computer and so they are required to access this information through use of the computer keyboard. Other people move into the world of computer programming and find they have to input their programs by use of the computer keyboard. Many students find it useful to type their notes, essays, and theses. Children and parents take an interest in computing and so use the computer keyboard as part of their hobby or pastime. It is predicted that in future some of our shopping will be carried out through use of a keyboard whilst sitting in the comfort of our homes.

However, keyboarding involves more than just typing, it also involves display of information directly on paper when using a typewriter or data on a VDU screen followed by printing from the computer. It seems logical that we should all learn how to use the keyboard accurately and efficiently in order to display text and numerical data effectively on the page.

Chapter 1

The Equipment

Handwriting is the commonest way of recording information on paper or of passing information on to another person, but we all know that handwriting is a slow method of recording information, and it may be difficult to read. Machines have been introduced to overcome these problems. This chapter briefly describes the various types of machine available.

1.1 Typewriters

Manual typewriters

The original typewriters and their modern counterparts are a single piece of machinery of which the following basic parts are identifiable (Fig. 1):

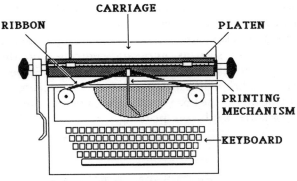

RIBBON   CARRIAGE   PLATEN

PRINTING MECHANISM

KEYBOARD

FIG 1   A Manual Typewriter

1   a keyboard
2   a platen (around which the paper rotates as it advances)
3   a mechanism known as the carriage, for
   (i)   advancing the paper around the platen
   (ii)   moving the typing point across the paper

1

    4   an inked or carbonised ribbon for depositing print on the paper
    5   a mechanism for impressing characters on the paper through the ribbon (printing mechanism).

The user (generally known as a typist) is required to depress a key which moves a mechanism containing a letter such as *a* (or a figure or symbol) to press the ribbon against a piece of paper so that the letter is printed on the paper. Because the whole operation is done manually such typewriters are termed 'manual typewriters'.

Electric typewriters

Manual typewriters were improved by the use of electricity to power the moving parts. The typist using an electric typewriter still has to press the keys but electricity causes the mechanical parts to print the letters on the paper. Some operations, such as inserting paper into the machine, may be done manually.

Electronic typewriters

It may be difficult for the newcomer to the field of typewriting to differentiate between an electric typewriter and an electronic machine (Fig. 2) because both are powered by electricity. The essential difference lies in the fact that an electronic typewriter contains a microprocessor to control the machine functions. In addition, there is no moving carriage; instead, the print head moves from left to right across the platen as keys are struck. Most electronic typewriters carry out extra functions such as automatic centring, underlining and emboldening of text, and automatic paper feeding. Some machines will also display a line of text in a small 'window', or screen, on the front of the machine before the text is printed on paper, so that the text may be altered or corrected before printing.

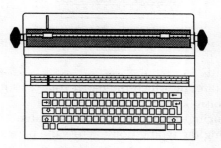

FIG 2   Electronic Typewriter

Electronic typewriters may also be equipped with memory facilities so that words, phrases or paragraphs of text may be stored and recalled for printing at a later date. A memory unit may be an integral part of the typewriter, or may be a separate unit linked to the machine by a cable.

1.2 Computers

A computer can carry out the same functions as a typewriter through the use of a word processing program. The program is known as *computer software*. Some computers are designed specifically to undertake the typewriting function and are used for no other purpose. These are known as *word processors*. They are computers 'dedicated' to word processing, which is why they are often referred to as 'dedicated word processors'. General purpose microcomputers are designed to carry out many functions, just one of them being word processing.

The computer consists of a number of separate pieces of equipment, although they may be housed in a single casing. These separate units consist of the following identifiable basic parts (Fig. 3):

1   the central processing unit (CPU) which controls the word processing program
2   an input device; for typing puposes this is generally a keyboard, but other methods of inputting text are available, most of which are not relevant to word processing
3   a visual display unit (VDU) which contains a screen for viewing what has been input
4   one or more disk drives, which allow the use of external memory storage systems in the form of a disk
5   the printer.

These are sometimes referred to as *hardware*.

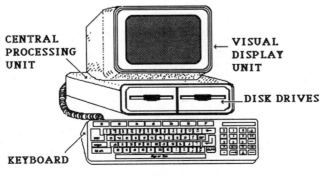

FIG 3   Microcomputer

1.3 Comparison of Typewriters with Computers

Typewriters and word processing programs used with a computer will carry out the same functions of printing words, figures and symbols on paper. They differ in 'how' and 'when' the words are printed.

The typewriter

Whenever a key is depressed on a manual typewriter a letter, figure or symbol is printed on paper immediately. To use a computing term, it is immediate *hard copy*.

A typing error must be corrected by rubbing out, painting out or 'lifting off' the incorrect letter and typing the correct letter in its place. If a paragraph needs to be moved on a page the whole page of text has to be re-typed. This process of correcting and re-typing is time-consuming and inefficient.

The computer

Whenever a key is pressed on a computer a letter, figure or symbol is input into the computer and is displayed on the screen of the VDU. This display is termed *soft copy*.

Soft copy may be read on the screen and changed, or edited, by deleting incorrect letters (using appropriate keys on the keyboard) and inserting the required letter. Paragraphs may be moved within a page of text or between pages, which eliminates the need for re-typing. A computer can carry out some functions that cannot be carried out on a manual or electric typewriter, e.g.

1   centre, underline and embolden text automatically
2   search for particular words or phrases and replace them with other words and phrases
3   store large amounts of text which are frequently used (such as standard letters) so that they can be recalled and inserted into another document
4   divide a document into page lengths after it has been typed, but before it is printed out
5   copy text.

When the text has been input, it is saved to an external storage device (such as a disk) and a hard copy printed. The stored text may be recalled to the screen at any time, then modified, re-saved and printed. This eliminates the need to re-type text and none of the corrections or amendments are apparent on the hard copy.

The electronic typewriter

Many electronic typewriters occupy a role somewhere between a manual or electric typewriter and a computer. They have a limited memory which allows a certain number of words to be input before giving the command to print on paper. They do not allow for movement of text throughout a page or between pages. When the text has been printed, editing of corrections is carried out in the same way as they are on an electric typewriter.

Some electronic typewriters may be linked to a computer so that the keyboard is used as the input device and the typewriter as the printer. This is a useful combination enabling an electronic typewriter to be upgraded so that it forms part of the computer's hardware.

Other electronic typewriters are equipped with disk drives for saving text, and a VDU screen for viewing text. This greatly improves the editing facilities of the typewriter, enabling the typist to amend text before it is printed.

1.4 What Does It Mean?

carriage A mechanism on a manual typewriter which contains the platen around which the paper is placed. The carriage moves from right to left as each letter is printed on the paper. The line space mechanism fitted to the carriage advances the paper by one or more line spaces when the return lever or return key is operated.

hard copy A 'print-out' of text from a computer or word processor.

platen A roller or cylinder on which the typing paper rests. Its rotation advances or reverses the paper, depending on which way the roller is turned.

ribbon A long, narrow strip of material impregnated with a print medium. When the printing mechanism of a typewriter or printer strikes the ribbon, the print medium is deposited on the typing paper. There are two major types of ribbon: (a) fabric ribbon (b) carbon ribbon.

soft copy Text displayed on the screen of a visual display unit. It is 'soft' in the sense that it is easily modified or corrected.

text Words or symbols displayed on the VDU screen or printed on paper.

window display   A 'thin' screen located just above the keyboard on some electronic typewriters in which a soft copy of text is displayed immediately it has been typed. The number of words displayed in the window is very limited, but it can be modified/corrected before being printed on paper.

Test Your Knowledge

1   Why is a manual typewriter so called?
2   Name the basic parts of a manual typewriter.
3   For what are the letters CPU an abbreviation?
4   Name three types of computer hardware.

(See p. 185 for the answers)

Activity

Reading about the various types of typewriter and computer is all well and good, but it will be helpful to you if you can identify the various machines. Your task is to identify and, if possible, to obtain advertising literature on manual, electric and electronic typewriters and at least one microcomputer, with its peripherals. You may carry out this activity on your own or as a member of a group.

There are various ways of going about your task: (a) look through magazines and cut out relevant advertisements or write away for information; (b) call in at your local office equipment and/or computer suppliers; (c) attend an exhibition. However, remember that printed advertising literature is expensive and suppliers of this type of equipment can justifiably become annoyed if too many individuals use up their supply of advertising material when they do not intend to buy the equipment.

Chapter 2

The Environment

Everything in the room in which we work makes up the workplace environment, and we obviously feel more at ease in a pleasant environment than in an unpleasant one. Various factors make up the environment.

2.1 The Factors

Decor

The colour of walls, ceiling and flooring should harmonise and make us feel at ease.

Lighting

Lighting is very important, because too much or too little light can lead to eye strain. Direct light (either natural or artificial electric light) should not shine directly on the work station. Sunlight shining on the copy paper or on the VDU screen can become glaring and cause difficulty in reading the text. An anti-glare screen can be fitted to the front of a VDU screen to help overcome this problem. Vertical blinds at a window are useful for controlling natural light (Fig. 4) and strip lighting is a useful means of artificial lighting.

Heating

The working environment should be sufficiently warm for comfort but should never become cold or overbearingly hot, either of which can cause discomfort.

Ventilation

A stuffy atmosphere can lead to drowsiness and loss of concentration, and a change of air in the room at regular intervals is essential. This can be achieved by simply opening a window or door for a short

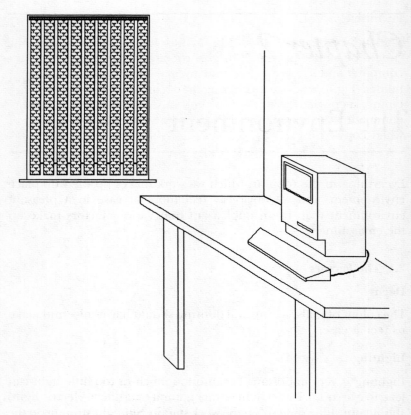

FIG 4   Vertical blinds control natural light.

period or by use of an extractor fan. Large offices may use air-conditioning which is programmed to change the air a given number of times each hour. Electronic air cleaners, sometimes referred to as ionisers, are also available for removal of 'stuffiness'. These are said to remove particles of dust, pollen and tobacco smoke from the air. At the same time it is claimed that they inject negative ions into the office to produce an invigorating atmosphere.

Noise

Noise control is necessary for relaxation. Noise can lead to headaches, irritability and occasionally to nervous disorders. It is difficult to control the noise made by typewriters, but the noise produced by a computer printer can be considerably reduced by housing the printer within an acoustic hood.

Furniture

The surface of tables should be made of non-glare material, and should be sufficiently large to give room for the typewriter, or the computer and its peripherals, and any papers being copied. A 'copy holder' (Fig. 5), a device for holding the documents being copied when typing, keeps papers off the desk and raises them to 'eye level', thus eliminating the continual head movements from table top to screen when 'copy typing'.

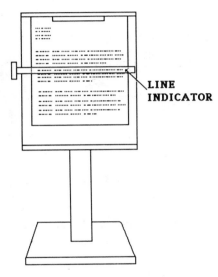

LINE
INDICATOR

FIG 5   Copy holder

The height of the table is linked with seating. The top of the table should be about level with the typist's elbows, so that the keyboard can be operated comfortably. The height of the chair should be adjustable so that the typist can sit with feet resting comfortably on the floor.

Ideally, the seat needs an adjustable backrest, to support the back in an upright position, so that the typist can sit comfortably for what may be fairly long periods of time. The chair should be so adjusted that the typist can maintain the ideal sitting position for typing throughout the working day. The ideal sitting position (Fig. 6) includes:

1   feet resting on the floor, slightly in front of the body and with one foot a little forward
2   thighs about parallel with the floor

3 arms rising slightly from the elbow to bring the forearms parallel to the slope of the keys on the keyboard, (some computer keyboards have little or no slope); the height of the chair should be adjusted to give the required slope to the forearms
4 elbows taking up a restful position near the body
5 the body leaning forward slightly with the back supported by the backrest of the chair.

FIG 6 Sitting position at the keyboard.

Equipment

The keyboard should be parallel with the edge of the table with the typist sitting directly in front of it. This is relatively simple when using a typewriter but it may not be easily achieved with a microcomputer if the keyboard is built into the visual display unit. The position of the VDU screen controls the angle of the keyboard in relation to the operator. The VDU screen should be within reasonable viewing distance of the typist, preferably directly in front. However, the position of the VDU may depend on the length of cable between the VDU, CPU, disk drive, printer and the space available on the table top. Consequently, the VDU may have to be placed to the left or right of the keyboard. Necessity and comfort for looking at the screen may dictate that a typist should sit at a slight angle to the table and that the keyboard be at an angle to the edge of the table. However, ideally the typist should sit directly facing the desk (Fig. 7).

FIG 7   Relationship of typist to table and computer.

2.2 What Does It Mean?

acoustic hood   A specially designed box in which a printer is housed.
It deadens the sound of the printer. A clear plastic lid allows access
for removal of paper.

anti-glare screen   A special screen which is fitted to the front of a
VDU screen. It is said to reduce glare from the VDU screen, thereby
making reading from the screen easier and less tiring.

copy holder   A device for holding the copy paper whilst the text is
copied. It holds the copy at eye level and many copyholders have a
means by which the line being copied is highlighted.

copy paper   Paper on which text is written, typed or printed and
which the typist copies.

copy typing/typist   The process of copying text by typing. A person
who copies written, typed or printed text is known as a *copy typist*.

electronic air cleaner   A device for freshening the air of a room. It is
said to remove minute particles of dirt, pollen and smoke from the
atmosphere.

electrostatic field   Some anti-glare screens are also said to reduce
the electrostatic field emitted by the VDU screen. Some people
claim that this electrostatic field can cause irritation of the eyes, dry
skin and possibly itchy rashes.

ergonomics   The study of man and his environment in order to
make the environment harmonise with the person so that he or she
can work at maximum efficiency.

workstation   The table at which the typist sits. The term is used in
computing to refer to the siting of a single VDU and keyboard.

Test Your Knowledge

1 What are the advantages of fitting an anti-glare screen to a visual display unit?
2 What methods are available for ventilating a room?
3 How may printer noise be minimised in an office?
4 Describe the ideal arm position when typing.

(See p. 185 for the answers)

Activity

Draw up a table, like that shown below, listing the factors which make up the working environment in the room in which you are learning to type. Include columns indicating whether you consider the environmental factors as excellent, very good, good, poor, non-existent.

	Excellent	Very Good	Good	Poor	Non-existent
Decor					
Lighting					
etc, etc.					

Having done this, carry out a survey of your working environment by placing a tick in the boxes. When your survey has been completed, write a short report outlining the good points about your working environment and indicate where you think improvements could be made.

Chapter 3

Preparing the Machine

3.1 Typewriters

The process of printing on paper is immediate on a typewriter, therefore it is necessary to insert paper in the machine before starting to type.

Preparing the manual typewriter

Set the paper guide at the '0' position on the scale located on the paper rest and raise the paper bail away from the platen (Fig. 8).

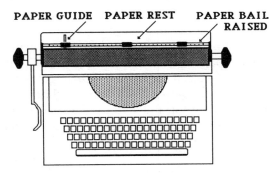

FIG 8   Set the paper guide at the '0' mark on the paper rest and raise the paper bail.

Inserting paper in the manual typewriter

Place a backing sheet behind the paper on which you are about to type. Hold the paper with the finger tips of both hands so that the backing sheet is facing you.

Place the paper between the paper rest and the platen and gently push it down until it will go no further. Use one hand to support the paper whilst the other rotates the platen knob (Fig. 9). Most typists use the left hand to support the paper whilst the right hand rotates the

13

platen knob to rotate the paper around the platen. As the paper appears on the keyboard side of the platen, guide the paper by hand between the platen and the paper bail.

FIG 9   Inserting paper into a typewriter.

Straightening the paper (paper alignment)

Rotate the platen knob until the paper behind the platen is about half an inch longer than the amount of paper in front of the platen (Fig. 10). Lower the paper bail onto the paper and gently press the front portion of the paper against the back portion of paper to check the alignment of the paper. If the left and right edges of the paper are exactly in line, the paper is straight. Alternatively the platen knob may be rotated further until the top and bottom edges of the paper touch. If the top and bottom edges are exactly in line with each other, the paper is straight.

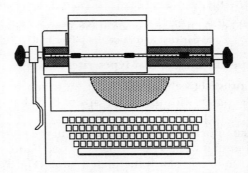

FIG 10   Checking the alignment of the paper.

Inaccurate alignment of the paper is usually due to the way the paper was inserted behind the roller in the first place. This can be corrected by activating the paper release lever and aligning the paper correctly as described above. Return the paper release lever to its original position. The paper is now correctly positioned in the machine.

Preparing electric and electronic typewriters

The method is the same as for manual typewriters.

Inserting paper in electric and electronic typewriters

The procedures for inserting paper into electric and electronic type-writers are often similar to a manual typewriter, but some machines are equipped with an automatic paper feed.

Automatic paper feed
A sheet of paper is inserted into the machine, against the paper guide in the same manner as described for the manual typewriter. The automatic paper feed lever is activated which causes the paper to be fed around the platen, automatically raising the paper bail to allow the paper to pass between the platen and the bail. When sufficient paper has been fed around the platen the paper feed lever is released. Paper alignment is corrected in the same manner as described for manual typewriters.

3.2 Computers

Before a computer can be used, the whole system must be switched on. Always switch on in the following order: (1) Printer; (2) VDU; (3) CPU. This minimises the possibility of an electricity surge damaging the CPU. Having switched the computer on, it needs to be prepared for use; this is known as 'logging on'.

Logging on procedures

The term 'log on' was originally used to describe the procedure by which a user would identify him/herself to the computer so that it would allow access to the program and data stored in its memory. The term generally referred to large mainframe and minicomputers, but it is often used nowadays to describe the process of loading a program into the memory of a microcomputer and preparing it ready for use.

A word processing program has to be loaded into the memory of the computer. This usually involves placing a word processing program disk in a disk drive and pressing the appropriate key or keys to allow the program to be loaded. Instructions about the procedures to be followed, known as *screen prompts* or *operator prompts*, may be displayed on the screen to help the typist.

The easiest word processing systems to use are those which are 'menu-based'. A *menu* displays a list of options such as: (1) create (or draft) a document; (2) edit a document; (3) save a document, etc (Fig. 11). The typist selects the function desired by moving the cursor to the appropriate option and pressing the relevant key.

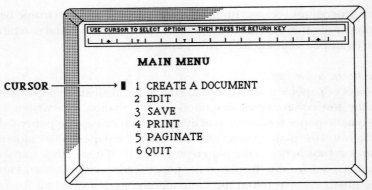

FIG 11   A menu displayed on the screen of a VDU.

In the context of this book the typist would select the option for creating (or drafting) a new document. This will usually present a clear screen, with the exception of a status line displayed at the top or bottom of the screen. The *status line* (see Fig. 20, p 33), which gives information to the typist, is explained more fully in Section 3.4.

The printer

The printer must also be prepared for use by ensuring that it is loaded with paper.

Inserting paper into the printer

There are three ways of inserting paper into a printer:

1   a single sheet at a time—manually
2   a single sheet at a time—automatically
3   automatic feed of continuous stationery.

Single sheet feed—manual
Most printers will allow paper to be fed in a single sheet at a time. The process is similar to that used for manual typewriters.

Single sheet feed—automatic
A hopper or sheet feeder may be fitted to a printer, which automatically feeds paper to the roller, one sheet at a time. A quantity of paper is placed in the hopper and the platen knob is rotated to feed the first sheet of paper around the platen. The top margin position is set. Paper is automatically fed around the platen, one sheet at a time. The printed sheet is deposited in a tray above the platen and another piece of paper is automatically fed around the platen ready to print the next page of text. The printer is put 'on line' by pressing the appropriate key to allow the printer to accept signals from the computer.

Continuous stationery
Some printers are designed solely for the use of continuous stationery (Fig. 12) by means of a tractor feed mechanism. Continuous stationery is fed around the platen by sprockets (pins) entering holes on the edges of the paper (Fig. 13); as the platen rotates the paper is fed around the platen.

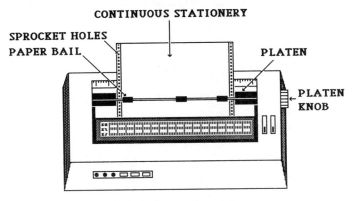

FIG 12 Computer printer.

In order to load the paper, the lid of the printer may have to be raised or removed and the paper bail raised. Paper is fed onto the sprockets and the platen knob rotated until the leading edge of the paper is in advance of the paper bail, which is then returned to rest on the paper. The leading edge of the paper is passed through the lid of the printer and the lid replaced. The position of the paper is adjusted so that the leading edge is in line with the top edge of the lid. The printer is put 'on line' ready for use.

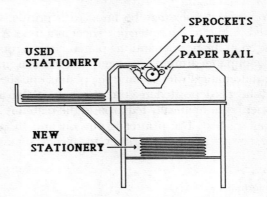

FIG 13   The flow of continuous stationery.

The computer is now at the same stage as the typewriter when paper had been loaded into it. The process of getting ready to type is more complicated with a computer than a typewriter, but the computer has many advantages when inputting and manipulating text.

3.3 Types of Printer

There are many types of printer, the main categories being:

1   thermal
2   dot matrix
3   daisy wheel
4   ink jet
5   laser.

Each of these differ in the way they print letters on the paper. The most commonly used printers for word processing purposes are dot matrix and daisy wheel printers.

3.4 What Does It Mean?

automatic paper feed   Most electronic and some electric type-writers have a mechanism for automatically feeding paper around the platen. The switch used to activate this function is generally found behind the paper release lever, on the left of the machine.

backing sheet Most typists use two pieces of paper when typing. The front sheet is the one on which text is printed. The back sheet (which should be slightly thicker than the front sheet) is used to protect the platen and thereby increases its life. It is termed the backing sheet. The two sheets must be the same size and exactly aligned.

continuous stationery A long length of paper folded and generally serrated into page lengths. The paper is automatically fed around the platen by pins (at each end of the platen) entering holes in the left and right borders of the paper.

hopper or sheet feeder A hopper or sheet feeder is a mechanism for storing paper above the platen and for collecting paper as typing is completed. It allows a single sheet of paper to be fed around the platen automatically and receives each sheet of paper as typing/printing is completed.

log-on The term log-on was originally used to describe the procedure by which a user would identify him/herself to the computer so that it would allow access to the program and data stored in its memory. The term generally referred to large mainframe and minicomputers. It is often used nowadays to describe the process of loading a program into the memory of a microcomputer and preparing it ready for use.

log-off The name given to the procedure of leaving the program.

menu-based system A menu is a display of functions shown on the VDU screen. The typist selects the appropriate function by typing a number or letter or by moving the cursor to the required function on the screen and pressing the enter key. These are the easiest systems to use.

on-line On-line means that the peripheral device (printer, etc.) is waiting instructions from the CPU.

off-line Off-line means that the peripheral is not 'listening' to the CPU. It could possibly mean that the printer is not switched on.

paper bail The paper bail is a bar, usually fitted with small rollers, used to hold the paper firmly against the platen on the keyboard side of the roller. The bail needs to be raised off the platen before paper is fed into the machine.

paper guide   The paper guide sets the position of the left hand edge of the paper in the machine so that when each new sheet is inserted the margins will be standardised. The paper guide is generally set at the '0' position on the scale which is located on the paper rest.

paper rest   Sometimes referred to as the *paper table*. It is an angulated metal plate found immediately behind the platen, against which the trailing section of the paper rests.

paper release lever   Paper is always held under slight pressure against the platen. This pressure may be released for the purpose of paper alignment, by activating the paper release lever. It is found on the left hand side of the machine, about level with the platen. It must be de-activated once the paper has been aligned.

platen knob   A knob on the outer extremities at each end of the platen. Rotation of the knob rotates the platen.

screen prompts   Sometimes referred to as *operator prompts*, they are instructions relating to procedures being carried out and are intended to help the typist. They are shown at the top or bottom of the VDU screen.

status line   The status line is shown at the top or bottom of the VDU screen. It indicates the state or status of the current document. The following factors may be displayed on the status line:

1   name of document and/or file
2   cursor point (position) across the line
3   page number/line number
4   whether in insert or edit mode
5   left and right margin settings
6   whether ragged or justified margins are in use
7   tab settings.

tractor feed   A mechanism of sprockets (pins) at each end of the printer platen on to which is fed continuous stationery.

Test Your Knowledge

1   What is the purpose of a backing sheet?
2   List the ways by which paper may be inserted into a computer printer.
3   What is meant by logging on procedures?

(See p. 185 for the answers)

Activity

Examine the machine you are about to use and determine how the paper is to be fed into the machine. Read the user manual and write notes on the procedure to be followed. Using your notes, feed the paper into the machine. Alternatively, work with a colleague and read out the instructions you have written down, whilst your colleague loads paper into the machine, following your instructions precisely. Then change over and follow your colleague's instructions to see if you can load paper into the machine correctly. Do remember to amend your instructions if you find they are incorrect or if sections are missing from them.

Chapter 4

Page Layout

Typing is not simply about printing text on a piece of paper. It is also about how that text looks when it is set out as a document. The typist is therefore concerned with 'page layout', which involves four main factors:

1 the size of paper being used
2 the type and size of the print to be used
3 the amount of space which should surround the text—the margins
4 the amount of space to be left between lines and sections of the text.

4.1 Paper Sizes

Various sizes of single sheet feed paper are available. The paper sizes most commonly used for typing are illustrated in Fig. 14. Paper can be used with the narrow edge at the top (*portrait*) or with the long edge at the top (*landscape*).

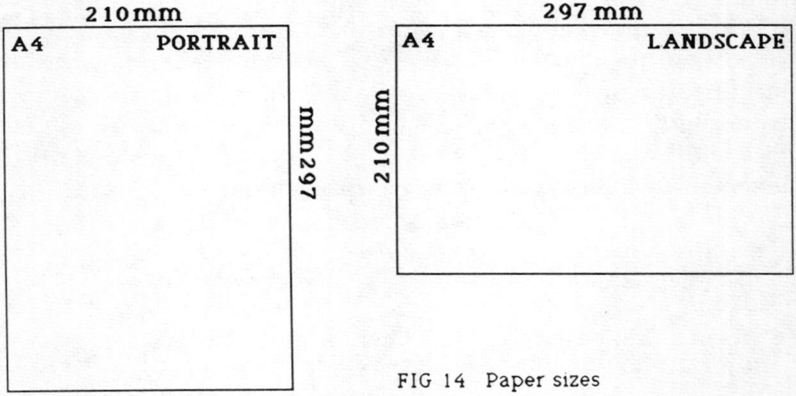

210mm
A4   PORTRAIT

297mm

mm297

297mm
A4   LANDSCAPE

210mm

FIG 14   Paper sizes

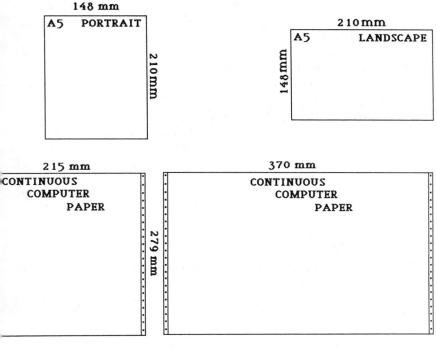

FIG 14 Paper sizes

4.2 Types of Print

Print comes in numerous styles and sizes. In printers' terms (i.e. people who print books or newspapers) it is referred to as *fonts* and *points*. A font is the style or shape of the print, whilst points refers to the size of the print. Many computer manufacturers use the printing terms, and it is possible for the typist to change the fonts and points before printing. Different terms are used to describe the same features on typewriters. Instead of points, the sizes of the print, known as Elite, Pica and Micro, are given in terms of *pitch*, which is the number of letters that can be typed within the space of one inch.

```
Pica 10 pitch = 10 letters to the inch

Elite 12 pitch = 12 letters to the inch

Micro 15 pitch = 15 letters to the inch
```

With each of these type sizes the space taken up by an individual letter is the same, no matter what letter of the alphabet is typed.

An alternative type size is known as *proportional spacing*, where the space taken up by a single letter is proportional to the size of the letter. The letter *i* takes up less space than the letter *m* or *w*, and this gives the completed work the appearance of material produced by a printer of books.

Manual typewriters and most electric machines have fixed typestyles. They are bought with an Elite or Pica typeface and this cannot be changed. Some electric and all electronic typewriters allow the operator to change the typestyle by use of interchangeable typeheads. They may also allow the use of proportional spacing. Some computer printers also use interchangeable typeheads and proportional spacing.

4.3 Decisions

Before starting work the typist has to make the following decisions regarding type size and paper size:

1   select the style and size of type to be used (this is predetermined with manual typewriters)
2   analyse the amount of text to be typed
3   decide on the way in which the text is to be presented (e.g. letter, table of figures, etc.)
4   decide on which paper size to use (this will generally be A4 size)
5   decide on whether the paper is to be used portrait or landscape way.

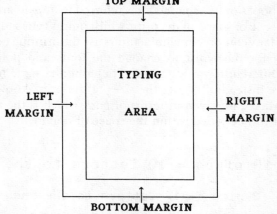

FIG 15   Margin positions and typing area.

4.4 Margins

Having made the above decisions it is possible to concentrate on positioning the text on the page by setting the margins. There are four margins to be considered: top, bottom, left and right (Fig. 15).

It is difficult to be specific about the size of margins to use, because much depends upon what is being typed. A general rule is to have all margins equal. Where possible they should be one inch wide (25 mm) but in certain circumstances they can be reduced to as little as half an inch wide (13 mm). If this generalisation is modified, the top and left margins are usually set to the same measurements, the typist adjusting the right and bottom margins to suit the text being typed.

Setting the top margin

Manual typewriter
Having inserted the paper into the manual typewriter and checked the alignment of the paper, it is possible to set the top margin. The paper bail is raised off the paper and the movement of the paper reversed to bring the top edge of the paper level with the typing point. This is done by reversing the movement of the platen knob.

Now the paper is advanced seven clear line spaces by use of the carriage return lever. Using the inside edge of the index finger of the left hand, the carriage return lever is moved towards the body of the typewriter until it will go no further. Each time this is done the paper moves forward (upwards) one line and the typing point moves to the left margin (see line spacing). The paper bail is lowered onto the paper.

Electric and electronic typewriters
The top edge of the paper is set at the typing point in the same manner as for manual typewriters. Advancement of the paper is accomplished by pressing the return or line spacing function key. This key is usually termed the *return key*. It may have the word RETURN, ENTER or an arrow ← printed on it. Each time the return key is pressed the paper will advance by one line and the typing point will move to the left margin. The key is pressed seven times to give a top margin of six clear line spaces or one inch (25 mm).

Computers
Many word processing programs used on a computer have a pre-set top margin of six or seven clear line spaces. This is known as a *default*

setting. The top margin is not visible on the VDU screen, but the paper automatically advances six or seven clear line spaces before the printer begins to print.

The default setting can be changed to suit the requirements of the typist by selecting from the options in the menu. Additional line spaces may be inserted without altering the default setting by simply pressing the return key. These line spaces are shown on the screen.

Setting the bottom margin

Manual/electric/electronic typewriters

The simplest way for the beginning typist to establish the bottom margin with any typewriter is to mark the margin position on the paper before inserting it into the machine. Measure one inch (25 mm) up from the bottom edge of the paper and make a small pencil mark on the right or left edge of the paper. Make a further mark at one and a half inches (38 mm) up the paper. When the first mark comes into view, the typist knows that three more lines (of single line spaced typing) may be typed before reaching the bottom margin position. The pencil marks must be rubbed out after typing the page of text.

As an alternative thick black lines may be ruled on the *backing sheet* one inch and one and a half inches (25 mm and 38 mm) from the bottom edge of the paper (Fig. 16). These lines will show through the typing paper so that the approach of the bottom margin position can be seen.

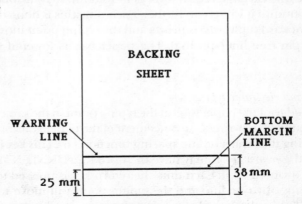

FIG 16   Bottom margin line and warning
line drawn on a backing sheet.

Computer

Word processing programs used on a computer have a pre-set bottom margin (a *default setting*), which may be indicated on the VDU screen as a broken line. The computer system 'knows' how many lines should be allowed to a page, and the broken line indicating the bottom margin is known as a *soft page break*. On many word processing programs the program automatically moves the next section of text on to the following page when one page is full. On others a *pagination* procedure is necessary. The pre-set page length may be modified to suit the work being typed by adjusting the default setting. Alternatively, most programs allow the operator to override the soft page break by inserting a 'hard' page break wherever it is required (within the length of the pre-set page).

Setting left and right margins

Manual typewriter

The left margin is set by depressing the left margin stop, located behind the paper rest. It is then moved to the required position and released. When a one inch (25 mm) left margin is required, the margin is set as shown in Fig. 17. The same procedure is used to set the right margin by backspacing from the right hand edge of the paper.

A bell will sound when the typing point is about ten letters from the right margin stop. This is a warning that the right margin is near and these last ten character spaces are known as the *bell zone*. The carriage return lever must be operated to return the typing point to the left hand margin and to advance the paper by one line ready for the next line of type.

If the word being typed is too long to fit on the line within the set margins, the typist may either split the word, and take part of the word down on to the next line (see p. 149), or press the margin release key, which allows typing to continue into the right margin space.

Electric and electronic typewriters

The existing margin may have to be cancelled by pressing the appropriate key. The printing point is moved to the right by tapping the space bar, or is moved to the left by tapping the backspace key. When at the required position (see Fig. 17) the left hand margin stop (or set) key is pressed. The same process is repeated for the right margin, but this time the right hand margin stop key is pressed.

Electric typewriters, and most electronic machines, require the typist to press the carriage return lever when within the bell zone. However, some electronic typewriters may automatically return the carriage and advance the paper by one line when the typing point enters the bell zone.

Margin Settings on A4 Paper—Portrait

LETTERS ACROSS PAGE	80		100		124	
PITCH	10		12		15	
MARGINS	Left	Right	Left	Right	Left	Right
½″	5	75	6	94	7	117
1″	10	70	12	88	15	109
1½″	15	65	18	82	22	102
2″	20	60	24	76	30	94
2½″	25	55	30	70	37	87
3″	30	50	36	64	45	79

Line Lengths on A4 Paper—Portrait

PITCH	10		12		15	
MARGINS	Left	Right	Left	Right	Left	Right
LINE LENGTH						
40 letters	20	60	30	70	42	82
44 letters	18	62	28	72	40	84
50 letters	15	65	25	75	37	87
55 letters	12	67	22	77	34	89
60 letters	10	70	20	80	32	92

FIG 17

Margins for exercises

When you are typing exercises from Chapters 8 to 35 you will be given instructions to use a particular 'line length' rather than margin sizes. This is simply because the margins vary depending on the size of type used, and it is easier to ask you to use a line length of, for example, 50 letter spaces. Refer to the second table in Fig. 17 for guidance on line lengths for the various type sizes.

Computers
There are various ways of setting left and right margins on computers. Most have default settings which may be adjusted by the operator. This is generally done through a ruler line displayed on the screen of the VDU (Fig. 18). The typist types appropriate letters such as *L* for left and *R* for right at the desired positions on the ruler line.

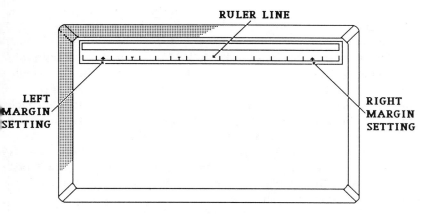

FIG 18   Ruler line showing left and right margin settings.

Some systems may require the operator to give a 'command' (an instruction) such as L10 for a left margin of ten letter spaces and R70 for a right margin of ten letter spaces. These margin settings would give one inch margins and a line length of 60 letters on an A4 sheet of paper with Pica 10-pitch type. The margin settings are usually activated by pressing the return key (or enter key) to input the command into the memory of the computer.

The computer equivalent of 'carriage return' is automatic on the VDU screen. Some word processing packages will split a word when it reaches the margin, part of the word being on one line and the rest of the word on the next line. However, most word processing programs do not split words at the end of a line; instead they automatically move the whole word onto the next line—a process known as *word wrap* or *wraparound*. The line endings inserted by automatic 'carriage returns' are known as *soft returns*. A typist may insert a line ending by pressing the return or enter key whenever necessary (e.g. at the end of a paragraph) and this is known as a *hard return*.

Printing is carried out in accordance with the instructions given to the computer, usually through a print menu. Printing routines vary from system to system, and the operator should always check the operating manual for the correct instructions.

4.5 Line Spacing

Line spacing refers to the amount of space left between lines of text. Variation of line spacing is used to create a pleasing display, or layout, of the text. It is also useful to have extra clear line spaces between lines of type when the document is to be read (e.g. a speech), or sent to a printer for print-setting, or when the text is likely to be altered (e.g. a draft document).

The usual line spacings are 1, 1.5, 2, 2.5 and 3, the most commonly used being 1, 1.5 and 2. On setting 1, the text will be printed in single line spacing. Print will follow on the next line. Setting 1.5 is known as one-and-a-half line spacing, and this leaves half a clear line space between lines of type. Setting 2, double line spacing, leaves one clear line space between lines of type.

On most fairly modern typewriters the line spacing mechanism is graduated in half line spaces. By turning the platen knob, the typist can override the line space setting and advance the line spacing by half a line space, if desired.

Manual typewriters

On most manual typewriters a scale marked 1, 1½ and 2, indicates the chosen line space setting, and a small lever is moved against the desired setting. One single operation of the carriage return lever will then advance the paper by 1, 1½ or 2 line spaces, depending on the setting chosen. Some manual typewriters, particularly small portable machines, are fitted with only single line spacing. To type in double line spacing it is necessary to operate the carriage return lever twice.

Electric and electronic typewriters

Electric and electronic typewriters have a lever or key to select the desired line spacings, and the paper is automatically advanced by the chosen amount when the return key is pressed.

Computers

With word processing programs on computers, line spacing may be set either through a menu or on the ruler or status line. On most systems text will be displayed on the screen in single line spacing even when double line spacing has been chosen, but the text will be printed in the chosen line spacing. Other programs have a 'What You See is What You Get' approach (abbreviated to WYSWYG), and text is displayed on the screen exactly as it will be printed out, including the display of the selected line spacing.

4.6 What Does It Mean?

bell zone An area of about ten letters length which exists between a bell sounding and the right hand margin on a typewriter. The bell warns the typist that action needs to be taken to return the typing point to the left margin.

carriage return function The carriage return lever on a manual typewriter and the return key or line spacing function key on electric and electronic typewriters and computers carry out the same function. It moves the typing point/cursor point to the left margin and at the same time advances the paper by one line, or moves down the VDU screen by one line.

cursor The cursor is a line or block (sometimes flashing or blinking) displayed on the screen of the VDU (Fig. 20, p. 33). It indicates the typing position on the screen. The cursor can be moved around the screen by use of the cursor movement keys which are generally found to the right of the QWERTY keyboard (Fig. 25, p. 47). Some programs use the QWERTY keys in conjunction with function keys to carry out movement of the cursor (e.g. ALT plus S may move the cursor one space to the left).

default settings Many word processing programs have margins, line spacing, etc. preset by the programmer. These default settings may be altered by the typist, but failure to do so results in the pre-set settings being used.

hot zone A computer term similar in meaning to the bell zone on a typewriter. A bell does not sound but the computer makes decisions about movement of a word onto the next line and insertion of a soft return.

interchangeable typeheads or printheads   Electric and electronic typewriters and some printers have the facility for changing the font and point size of the typehead. One typehead is removed and replaced by another. They are referred to as interchangeable typeheads or interchangeable printheads.

margin release key   It is possible to type within the left or right margins by activating the appropriate margin release key, which overrides the margin setting on typewriters. The procedure lasts for one line only and has to be repeated on each subsequent line if required.

page break—hard   This is a page break (the end of a page) set by the typist. The typist instructs the computer to insert a page break. They remain operative no matter how much the text is changed, until the typist instructs the computer to delete the hard page break and return to soft page breaks.

page break—soft   A word processing program may automatically divide a long document into pages of a specific length. The end of the page is shown by spaced dashes, or some other symbol, across the screen. The position of these soft page breaks is automatically changed by the computer if changes are made to the text.

pagination   The process of dividing a document into page lengths. Some word processing packages paginate automatically.

return—hard   All carriage returns on a manual typewriter are hard returns. The typist has to insert one at the end of each line. Similarly on a computer, a hard return is one inserted by the typist. It remains in the text until the typist instructs the computer to remove it.

return—soft   A carriage return inserted at the end of a line by a computer. It is automatically adjusted by the computer as text is altered.

ruler line   A ruler line refers to a line divided into letter widths and shown on a VDU screen (Fig. 18, p. 29). Margins and tab-stops may be set on it. The ruler line may be permanently displayed or recalled to screen when required. A ruler, or paper scale, is permanently displayed on the paper rest of a manual and electric typewriter. Many electronic typewriters feature a transparent scale, showing three different pitch sizes; the typing point is indicated by a pointer moving behind the transparent scale.

typing point   The position on paper (sometimes called the printing point) at which the next letter (figure, symbol) is to be printed (Fig. 19). The term cursor position is used for the same purpose on screen based systems (Fig. 20).

wordwrap or wraparound   A procedure carried out by a computer which automatically takes a word down to the next line should it be too long for the first line.

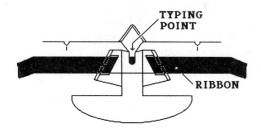

FIG 19   Typing point.

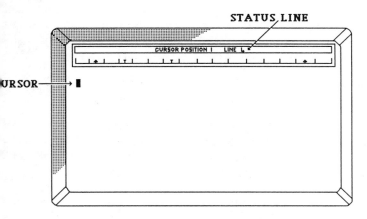

FIG 20   VDU screen showing cursor position and status line.

Test Your Knowledge

1   What is meant by a print font?
2   What words are used to describe the size of print?
3   List the most commonly used line spacings.
4   How does proportional spacing differ from standard spacing?

(See p. 186 for the answers).

Activities

1   Take two pieces of A4 plain paper and place them on a table so that one piece lies in a portrait position and the other in a landscape position. Write 'A4 Portrait' on the top edge of the paper which is lying portrait way and 'A4 Landscape' on the one that lies landscape way. File these samples in your folder as a reminder.

2   Check with your operating manual to see which font and points are being used on your machine. Consult your user manual to see the method of changing these typestyles and type sizes, if this is possible on your equipment.

Chapter 5

Proof-reading and Corrections

Proof-reading is a word borrowed from the printing trade. The 'proofs' are the first printed copy of a book, which must be read through carefully by the editor and the author to ensure that any errors are found and corrected.

When your page of text is produced on the typewriter or computer printer it also needs to be read for errors. The main difference between using a typewriter and using a word processing program on a computer is that the typist has the opportunity to proof-read and check work on the VDU screen. By proof-reading the soft copy on the screen, errors can be identified and corrected before printing takes place, thus saving the time that would be needed for re-printing.

5.1 How Errors Occur

The initial reason for proof-reading is to ensure the absence of errors. At the learning stage it also offers the learner an opportunity to analyse the reason for any errors. There are many causes such as loss of concentration through tiredness, interruptions from the telephone, or distractions from other people. Alternatively, the learner may not have established the correct finger reaches. The following is a guide to how errors may occur when learning to type.

All keyboards
1   The wrong letter has been typed.
    This is a common error when starting to type. It probably means that the correct finger reaches for those letters on the keyboard have not yet been learnt properly. Don't be afraid to look at the keys when typing in the early stages. This will help to give you confidence in reaching for the keys. It is better to look at the keyboard and reach

confidently in the right direction than to insist on keeping your eyes away from the keyboard and either moving the finger in the wrong direction, or wavering from one direction to another before finding the correct key. However, as you gain confidence, aim to keep your eyes on the exercise you are copying instead of on the keyboard.

Manual typewriter

1   Ghosting of the letters (Fig. 21).

Unless there is a fault on the machine, you are probably keeping the key depressed after striking it. Practise sharp, firm striking movements, remembering to remove finger pressure immediately the key has been depressed.

2   Dark and light letters (Fig. 21).

This is an indication of uneven striking, which is more likely to occur with the third and little fingers. This fault can be improved by typing with a regular rhythm until correct finger movements have been established.

JJ J   Ghosting

UNEVEN   Dark and Light Letters

AAAAA   Repeated letters

FIG 21   Common typing errors.

Computer

1   A single letter repeated (Fig. 21).

The finger has rested on an automatic repeat key too long. Use a sharp, definite finger action and raise the finger fractionally from the key as soon as it has been depressed so that the fingers 'hover' over the home keys.

5.2 Stages in Proof-reading

There are three stages involved in the process of proof-reading, which you may remember by the four 'Cs'—Correctness, Completeness, Comparison and Co-operation. The extent to which you use these proof-reading techniques will depend on the nature and purpose of the document you are typing.

Stage 1: Correctness and completeness

The document should be proof-read before it is removed from the typewriter, or from the screen before it is printed out if a computer is being used. If a typewriter is used, any errors may be corrected using the techniques described below under 'Correction of Errors'. If a computer is used, the hard copy should also be proof-read in case any errors have been overlooked during the screen check.

The text should be read carefully and checked to ensure that it is free from typographical and/or grammatical errors. Every word should be scanned to see that it is spelt correctly. Spaces between words should be checked. Numbers, symbols, capitalisation, underlining, line spacing and centring should all be checked.

Reading for typographical errors may not always identify any words or sentences that may have been omitted from the typescript. A sentence, or a whole document, may appear to be correct when read, even though a word or a whole paragraph has been omitted.

Stage 2: Comparison

The text (hard copy or soft copy) should be checked against the original. This may be done by reading a few words from the original, followed by reading the same section from the newly typed document. Always be aware of the fact that the eye will often read what it *expects* to see, which may be different from what is actually there.

Practise reading aloud, quietly. Read like a robot, without expression. Say precisely what is on the original, reading every character, including spaces, colon, comma, full stop, underline and so on. Even using this method it is possible to miss errors, especially on long complicated documents, or ones which contain many numbers. This is why Stage 3 is necessary.

Stage 3: Co-operation

It is important for typists to co-operate with colleagues in an office by helping with the proof-reading process. One person should read aloud from the original copy while the other checks the typed version. As the typist is the person responsible for the accuracy of what has been typed, it is important that the colleague reads aloud from the original using the technique described in Stage 2, while the typist checks the typed text. This is the only way for the typist to ensure that the colleague is concentrating all the time.

The task of proof-reading differs slightly between typewriter and computer. The text is originally read (Stage 1) whilst the paper is in the typewriter. With computers, the initial proof-reading of text is done from the screen. Proof-reading at Stages 2 and 3 is generally carried out when the paper has been removed from the typewriter or, if using a computer, after the text has been printed.

5.3 Correcting Errors

During the learning stages of keyboarding, the learner should not make any attempt to correct mistakes made. It is more important to identify what has *caused* those mistakes to happen, and to continue to practise correct finger reaches with further exercises. When competence at the keyboard has been achieved, the typist will wish to produce work that is free from any errors by correcting mistakes.

A competent typist is generally aware of typing an incorrect letter, immediately it is typed, and this ability will develop with experience. Errors should be corrected immediately, in case they are forgotten. Even though these known errors have been corrected, the text should still be proof-read for accuracy to identify any errors which may have been overlooked.

Manual, electric and electronic typewriters

Errors detected during Stage 1 of the proof-reading process are corrected whilst the paper is in the typewriter. There are various techniques for correcting errors:

Paint-out fluid   The paper is advanced so that the error is above the platen. This may be done by use of the carriage return lever, or by rotating the platen using the platen knob. Alternatively the carriage may be moved to the left or right to give access to the error.

A bottle of paint-out fluid is opened, excess fluid is removed from the brush and the fluid painted lightly over the incorrect letter. Care must be taken to ensure that no fluid drips onto the typewriter mechanism. When the liquid has dried, the deleted letter is returned to the typing point, and the correct letter typed.

Paint-out fluid is also available in the form of a pen, or a bottle with a pointed applicator, and these are used in much the same way as paint-out fluid applied with a brush.

Correction paper   Correction papers consist of small pieces of paper coated with a chalky white substance that is used to cover over incorrectly typed characters. Backspace the carriage until the typing point is over the incorrect letter. Place the correction paper between the typing paper and the ribbon and type the incorrect letter again. The incorrect letter will be covered by the correcting medium. Remove the correction paper, backspace and type in the correct letter.

Electric or electronic typewriters

Correction ribbon   Many electric and electronic typewriters are fitted with a correction ribbon. There are two types of correction ribbon: cover-up and lift-off.

Cover-up correction ribbon, used for corrections when typing with a fabric typing ribbon, is similar to correction paper in that the ribbon deposits a white substance over the incorrect letter. An error detected when typing is deleted by pressing the automatic correction key. The machine moves back along the line and the letter is deleted automatically. The machine remembers the letter previously typed. Memory is limited and relates only to what has just been typed. It is essential to check your machine manual for specific instructions.

Lift-off correction ribbon, used in conjunction with a carbon typing ribbon, is used in the same way as cover-up correction ribbon, but instead of the incorrect letter being covered over, the carbon deposit forming the incorrect letter is 'lifted off' the paper.

Computer

Typing errors may be corrected on the screen before the text is printed out. There are various ways of correcting errors:

1   the cursor is moved until it lies over the error and the delete key is pressed
2   the cursor is moved to the right of the incorrect letter and the 'backspace delete' key is used to delete the letter to the left of the cursor
3   the cursor is moved to the required position and the appropriate function key is used to delete a letter, word or words.

Having deleted the letter it is necessary to type the correct letter. Some systems may require the typist to change from 'overtype' mode to 'insert' mode to do this. Check your user manual for precise instructions on deletion and insertion of text.

5.4 Paper Removal

Manual typewriter

Use the right hand to move the 'paper release' lever forward to release the pressure rollers holding the paper in the roller and remove the paper from the machine.

Electric or electronic typewriters

Use the paper release lever and remove the paper, or use the automatic 'paper ejection' function.

Computer

If single cut sheets of paper are being used, the printer may automatically eject the paper; alternatively use the paper release lever and remove the paper from the machine by hand. If continuous stationery is used in your computer printer, press the form feed button to feed the paper into a position where you can tear off your printed sheet.

5.5 Corrections after Removal of Paper from the Machine

Typewriter

Obviously, once the paper has been removed from the typewriter, it is necessary to re-insert it into the typewriter if further corrections are to be made. Errors may be deleted by use of paint-out fluid before re-inserting the paper into the machine. The paper is inserted into the typewriter in the manner described on p. 13.

It is important to re-align the line of text accurately with the typing point (Fig. 19, p. 33). This may involve the use of the paper release lever and manipulation of the paper until the typing point is in the correct position. The alignment can be checked on the manual typewriter by *gently* tapping the correct letter key to give a faint image of the letter on the paper. If the alignment is correct, backspace and type the letter again.

Computer

A hard copy of a document obtained from a computer printer cannot be corrected in the manner described for typewriters. The document must be recalled to the screen and the delete/insert editing functions carried out to correct the text before re-printing.

5.6 Correction Signs

When a document has been typed it is usually returned to the originator for approval, and the final responsibility for the accuracy of the document rests with the author. The originator may have second thoughts about what was written and may wish to change the wording.

A range of commonly accepted correction signs are used to indicate any changes, and all typists should be aware of these. The typist may also use these signs when proof-reading during Stages 2 and 3 (see p. 37). The most frequently used correction signs are shown below:

ning	Sign	Example
rt a character, word, etc.	*ḷ*	by the desk *new*
·rt a space	# *ḷ*	and/the
·e up a space	*close up*	with͡out
capitals	*CAPS*	computer *CAPS*
upper case (capitals) ·ere indicated	*u. c.*	insert mode
spaced capitals	*sp. caps*	PRINTHEADS *sp. caps*
lower case letters	*l. c.*	PAGINATION
·he original word(s) stand	*stet* or Ⓥ	at the Factory works
·te the crossed out word(s)	*eu*	The old staff *eu*
·spose—change the position of ·e letters or words as indicated	*tr.*	ergonmdics in use the
·n a new paragraph where indicated · the square bracket	*N. P.*	place. ⌐If a
·on—do not start a new paragraph ·r join two paragraphs together)	*run on*	on paper. ⌐ At first the

5.7 What Does It Mean?

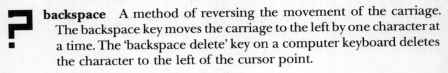

backspace   A method of reversing the movement of the carriage. The backspace key moves the carriage to the left by one character at a time. The 'backspace delete' key on a computer keyboard deletes the character to the left of the cursor point.

correction signs   These are symbols inserted in text by the proof-reader to indicate errors or changes required to the text.

insert mode   An instruction to the word processing program to insert letters as opposed to overtyping what is there.

overtype mode   When in overtype mode, the word processing program will type over (and therefore delete) any character where the cursor rests, replacing it with the newly-typed character.

proof-reading   A word borrowed from the printing trade, meaning the careful reading, correction and modification of the draft (first printed copy) of text.

Test Your Knowledge

1   What is meant by the term 'proof-reading'?
2   List the stages involved in proof-reading.
3   List three materials that may be used to delete typing errors.
4   Give the meanings of the following correction signs:

/   N.P.   stet

(See p. 186 for the answers)

Activity

The first passage of text shown below has been typed correctly. The second passage—which *should* be an exact copy—contains a number of typographical errors. Proof-read the second passage and indicate the errors by using correction signs. Check your work with the key on p. 187.

DRY TRANSFER LETTERING

We can all probably remember as children, getting coloured transfers which we moistened and placed on a hand or arm, pretending they were tattoos. These are known as wet transfers and they were also used commercially in graphics design.

A graphics designer, Dai Davies, developed a dry letter transfer which was marketed in 1962. It has changed the world of graphics design. Anyone can now insert professional-looking letters on diagrams and posters by simply rubbing a sheet to deposit the letter on paper. The number of fonts and points available is almost endless.

Dry Transfer Lettering

We can all probably remeber as children, getting coloured transfers which we moistened and placed on a hand or arm, pretending they where tattoos. These these are known as wet transfers and they were also used commercially in graphics design. A graphics designer, dai Davies, developed adry letter transfer which was marketed in 1926.

It has changed the world of graphics design. Anyone now can insert professional looking leters on diagrams and posters by simply rubbing a sheet to deposite the letter on paper The number of fonts and points available is almost endles.

Chapter 6

The Keyboard

6.1 The QWERTY Keyboard

Various forms of keyboard are available but this book is concerned with the QWERTY keyboard, which is illustrated in Fig. 22. There are four rows of keys, containing alphabet letters, numbers and symbols (or additional characters). The name QWERTY arises from the sequence of the alphabet keys at the left hand side of the third row. In addition, keyboards contain keys that carry out specific functions, such as the backspace, tab set and tab clear, shift key and shift lock, and the space bar.

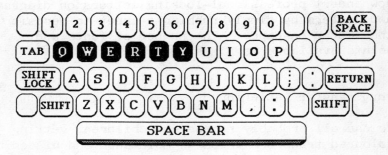

FIG 22   The QWERTY keyboard.

When a machine is described as having a QWERTY keyboard, it simply means that the arrangement of the alphabet letters on the bottom three rows of keys is standardised, whether it is a manual, electric or electronic typewriter, a dedicated word processor or a computer. On the second row of keys from the bottom, the keys **a s d f** and **j k l ;** are referred to as the *home keys* (Fig. 23). The significance of this is explained in Chapter 7.

44

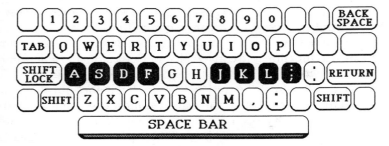

FIG 23   The home keys.

Figures 22 and 23 show the position of the *shift* and *shift lock* keys on a manual typewriter. Their position may vary slightly on other keyboards. Sometimes the shift key will be found alongside the space bar, with the shift lock next to the letter **z** key and a *caps lock* key next to the shift lock key. On many electronic keyboards a small red light indicates which of these keys is in use. The space bar, situated below the bank of QWERTY keys, inserts a space instead of a letter when it is depressed.

6.2 Number Keys

The top row of keys contains numbers ranging from 1 to 9 and then 0, their position being more or less standard throughout the range of machines. However, the position of fraction keys (e.g., ¼, ⅔, ½) may vary, particularly on electric and electronic keyboards. Many computer keyboards do not contain fraction keys, and if a ½ is required, the typist has to convert the figure to the decimal form, e.g., 0.5, or 1.5.

6.3 Symbol Keys

Symbols such as ? £ ( ), etc., are included on the number keys, and around the right hand side of the QWERTY keys. Unfortunately there is a very wide variation in the position of symbols on electric and electronic typewriters and on computer keyboards, and in the choice of symbols provided on the keyboard.

   Where a number and a symbol, or two symbols, are shown on one key, the upper symbol is typed by holding down the *shift key* and pressing the required key. On manual, electric and electronic typewriters, pressing the *shift lock* key also allows the symbols to be typed. Once the shift lock key has been depressed it remains active until the shift key is pressed to release it, and it is therefore used where a whole word, or several words, are required in capitals.

An additional key, the *caps lock* key, is usually fitted to computer keyboards. Its function is to convert all lower case alphabet letters into upper case letters (capitals) in the same way as the shift lock key. However, it differs from the shift lock key in that it does not affect the keys containing numbers, symbols and (in most cases) punctuation. When the caps lock has been depressed, the lower character of any two shown on a number or symbol key will be typed. This is particularly useful for people who are typing computer programs where capital letters and numbers are in constant use. The caps lock key must be pressed again to return to normal operation. Where a number and symbol, or two symbols, are shown on a key, the upper symbol can only be typed by pressing the shift key or shift lock.

Some electronic typewriters show three or four symbols on one key. The first two are accessed as described above. The third and/or fourth are accessed by pressing a special function key or control key. This special key may have to be pressed again to return to normal operation.

6.4 Numeric Key Pads or Number Pads

Many computer keyboards contain an additional key pad to the right of the QWERTY keyboard, which has the configuration of a calculator (Fig. 24). This is particularly useful to people who key in documents containing a lot of numbers. This key pad may also contain arithmetical function keys that allow the operator to carry out additions, subtractions, etc. In some cases the number key pad may consist of a separate small unit which is connected to the computer keyboard by means of a cable.

FIG 24   Numeric key pad

6.5 Additional Function Keys

Most electronic typewriters have additional keys which are used to carry out automatic functions such as centring, underlining, deletion of characters, etc. These may form an extra row of keys above the number row at the top of the keyboard, or they may be banked together to the left of the QWERTY keys, or between the QWERTY keys and the number pad.

Dedicated word processors and some computers have an additional key pad containing cursor movement keys, for moving the cursor around the screen (Fig. 25). Each key is labelled with an arrow indicating the direction of movement of the cursor—left, right, up and down, and on some keyboards an arrow pointing diagonally left that takes the cursor to the start of the document. Other special cursor movement keys may include movement of the cursor one word, sentence or paragraph at a time, to the end of the document, to the beginning of the document, to the end of a line, or to the beginning of a line. There may also be a special command key (action or execute key).

FIG 25 Cursor movement keys

Special function keys may also include centring, deletion, cut and paste, indent, search and replace, etc. On some computer keyboards the keys on the number row may be given additional functions when a special command, or alternative (ALT), key is pressed.

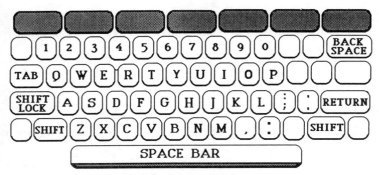

FIG 26 User defined keys

6.6 User Defined or Programmable Keys

Some computers have a fifth row of keys at the top of the keyboard (Fig. 26) which are termed *user defined* keys or *programmable* keys. The typist may program these keys to carry out specific functions similar to those described for dedicated word processors.

6.7 What Does It Mean?

numeric key pad   An additional grouping of numeric and function keys. It may form part of the keyboard or be an additional keyboard attached to the computer by a cable.

QWERTY keyboard   This type of keyboard is so called because, starting at the left hand side of the keyboard the first six keys on the top row of letters read QWERTY.

shift key   The shift key is used to change a single letter from a lower case letter (small letter) to an upper case letter (large letter or capital letter). The shift key is held down while the letter is typed and then released immediately.

shift lock   When the shift lock is depressed, all the alphabet letters on the keyboard are changed from lower case to upper case, and where a number and symbol, or two symbols, are shown on a key, the upper symbol will be typed.

caps lock   When the caps lock key is depressed, the alphabet letters are changed to upper case (capitals), but all other keys are unaffected.

user defined keys   A set of keys, generally at the top of the QWERTY keyboard, which may be programmed by the typist to carry out required functions.

Test Your Knowledge

1   Why is a QWERTY keyboard so called?
2   (a) How many shift keys are there on a QWERTY keyboard?
     (b) Where are the shift keys situated on the keyboard?
3   List four sets or banks of keys found on a keyboard.

(See p. 186 for the answers)

Activities

1   Draw a diagram of your keyboard and complete the diagram by inserting the letters, figures, etc. on each key.
2   If you are using a computer keyboard, experiment with the different uses of the shift key, shift lock and caps lock keys.

Chapter 7

Preparing to Type

Having carried out all the preliminary work, such as inserting paper into the typewriter or printer and logging on to the computer, you are ready to start typing.

7.1 Typing Position

Sit at the keyboard in the manner described on p. 9. Poise your hands over the home keys with the fingers slightly curved (Fig. 27). The wrists and forearms should be in a straight line, and the palms of your hands should not touch the typewriter or the desk at any point.

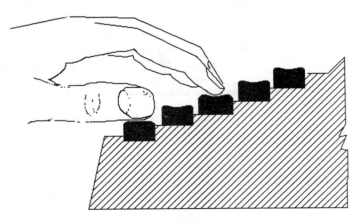

FIG 27   Finger position on the keys.

Position the index finger of the right hand over the letter **j**, and the index finger of the left hand over the letter **f**. The other fingers of your

49

left hand will then be positioned over **d, s** and **a**, while the other fingers of your right hand will be positioned over **k, l** and **;**. These eight keys are known as the home keys, because your fingers should always start from this position and return 'home' to them immediately after they have moved away to depress other keys.

7.2 Key Reaches

In 'touch typing', the fingers of both hands are each allocated certain keys (Fig. 28). The movement of a finger away from its home key to strike another key (and the return to the home key) is known as a *key reach*.

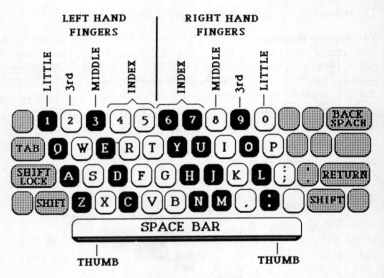

FIG 28 Key reaches.

7.3 Typing Action

Manual typewriter

The action of typing on a manual typewriter is firm, sharp and precise. Each finger in turn is used to give a sharp downwards tap on a key and immediately returned to the home position. Light pressure produces a faint letter impression on the paper. If a key is pressed too hard, or held down too long, a double image of the letter may be created on the paper (Fig. 21, p. 36).

Electric/electronic typewriters and computer

The action of typing on an electric/electronic typewriter or computer keyboard differs slightly from that used on manual typewriters. The keys of these keyboards are very sensitive and so require a lighter touch. The amount of pressure required varies between keyboards, and on many keyboards it is possible to change the sensitivity of the key response to suit the typist. Generally, however, a firm, light tapping action should be used. Pressure should be removed from the key immediately. As many keys on electronic keyboards have an automatic repeating action, failure to lift the finger from the key immediately may result in the letter being repeated across the page (electric/electronic) or the VDU screen (Fig. 21 p. 36).

7.4 Inserting Spaces with the Space Bar

Words are always separated from each other by a space. This is accomplished in typing by the use of the space bar. The space bar is generally the width of a row of letter keys. Its length gives freedom of movement of the hands, with the thumbs always able to strike the space bar whatever position the hand may be in. As a rule the right thumb is used to tap the space bar, but either thumb may be used. Some people alternate between the use of the left and right thumb, but it is generally considered better to use one thumb consistently. A firm, sharp tap should be used to depress the space bar.

7.5 Line Endings

Manual typewriter

When the end of a line is reached, it is necessary to move the typing point to the beginning of the next line, at the left margin. The fingers of the right hand are kept poised over the home keys, whilst the left hand is used to activate the carriage return lever. The action must consist of a single, firm and precise movement, otherwise the paper may not be advanced by a full line and the typing point will not be returned to the left margin.

Electric/electronic typewriters

The little finger of the right hand is used to depress the return key. The fingers of the right hand should be kept together in the slightly curved position, and the hand moved across to the right so that the little finger can press the return key. The hand should then immediately be returned to the home row position.

Computer

When a complete line of the screen of the VDU has been filled with text, the computer will automatically move the cursor point (typing point) to the left hand margin position on the next line through the automatic *word wrap* or *wraparound* function. If the line has not been filled, it will be necessary to depress the return key.

7.6 Typing Rhythm

Good typing comes from the development of a rhythm. It will be helpful at this stage in your learning to try to develop a rhythm. Say the letters to yourself as you type them, including the word space, to remind yourself that a space has to be inserted (e.g. *sss space lll space*). Keep the rhythm going when reaching the end of the line and using the carriage return lever or return key. Your accuracy is likely to improve by using this method, and it will help you to develop your typing speed. Experienced typists type to a rhythm, but not a strict metronomic rhythm. The rhythm of a competent typist depends upon the word and combination of letters being typed, and this develops with experience and practice.

7.7 Correction of Errors

When you are learning the key reaches, do not attempt to correct any errors you may make. Correction of errors takes up too much time and, more importantly, it interferes with the learning process. You are training your fingers to move in a particular direction for a specific distance. The important thing in the early stages is the accuracy of those key reaches and not what appears on the paper. If the key reach is correct, then the text printed on the paper will be correct.

Test Your Knowledge

1 List the letters which make up the home row of keys.
2 Why is the 'home' row of keys so called?
3 Describe the difference between the typing action required for a manual typewriter and that required for an electronic typewriter.

(See p. 186 for the answers)

Activity

Make a copy of the following checklist. Whenever you start typing, work through your checklist and ensure that you follow the suggestions made concerning these factors in this and previous chapters.

ERGONOMIC CHECKLIST									
Sitting Position Seat adjusted for height .... Seat adjusted for back support.									
Position of Feet Resting on the floor.............									
Position of Hands and Arms Hands poised over home keys .									
Fingers slightly curved..........									
Arms rising slightly									
Wrists straight									
Elbows close to sides............									
Back supported by backrest									
Position of Keyboard Parallel with the edge of the table...............................									
Lighting Correct intensity and direction.									
Heating Comfortable temperature.......									
Ventilation Room adequately ventilated....									

Chapter 8

The Use of Keys j and f

8.1 Introduction

Typing may be carried out in upper case letters (CAPITALS) or lower case letters (small letters). On a manual typewriter the shift key and shift lock key are used to type the upper case letters.

Some computer keyboards contain an additional caps lock (capitals lock) key for typing capital letters. The shift lock and caps lock keys are usually located on the left hand side of the keyboard. They act like a light switch in that they are 'on' or 'off'.

The first exercises contain only lower case letters. You should therefore ensure that the shift lock and caps lock keys are in the 'off' position—many computers have indicator lights to indicate when the shift or caps lock keys are 'on'.

8.2 Guidelines

1 Look at the keyboard and identify the home keys. They are ASDF on the left hand side of the keyboard and JKL; on the right hand side (see Fig. 23 p. 45). Poise your fingers over these keys, with the index finger of the right hand on the letter **j** key

and the index finger of the left hand on the letter **f** key. Both thumbs should be resting over the space bar, but exerting no pressure.

2 Take your fingers off the keyboard, look at the position of the home keys again and replace your fingers on the keyboard. Repeat this a number of times and then try to find the home keys without looking.

3 Look at the keyboard and identify the letter **f** and **j** keys. Place your fingers over the home keys and depress the letter **j** with the index finger of the right hand. Remember to release the key immediately after depressing it.

4 Press the space bar with your thumb after typing the letter **j**. Take your thumb off the space bar immediately after pressing it.

5 Repeat the process for the letter **f,** using the index finger of the left hand.

Computer printing
When you have typed the exercises it will be necessary to print a 'hard copy'. This is carried out in various ways depending upon the type of computer being used. Basically, printing may be done whilst the text is on screen by calling up a print menu, or by filing the text and giving printing commands from the main menu. Read the user manual for your particular machine before printing.

8.3 Exercises

For all exercises set single line spacing, and set a line length of 50 letter spaces (see p. 28 for guidance). Always allow for a top margin whenever you use a new sheet of paper (see p. 25).

Read through this chapter before starting to type, and follow the guidelines given. Insert paper into your typewriter or computer printer.

Exercise 1

1 Type one line of the letter **j**, pressing the space bar once after each letter.

2 At the end of the line press the return key.

3 Type one line of the letter **f**, pressing the space bar once after each letter.

4 At the end of the line press the return key.

5 Press the return key once more to insert an extra clear line space.

6 Repeat the exercise twice more.

Location Drills

j j j j j j j j j j j j j j j j j j j j j j j
f f f f f f f f f f f f f f f f f f f·f f f f

j j j j j j ´j j j j j j j j j j j j j j j j j
f f f f f f f´f f f f f f f f f f f f f f f f f

j j j j j j j j j j j j j j j j j j j j j j j
f f f f f f f f f f f f f f f f f f f f f f f

Exercise 2

Practise typing two letters followed by a space, and then three letters followed by a space. Type each line twice. Turn up an extra line space between each set of practice lines.

Location Drills

ff jj ff jj ff jj ff jj ff jj ff jj ff jj ff jj ff

jj ff jj ff jj ff jj ff jj ff jj ff jj ff jj ff jj

fff jjj fff jjj fff jjj fff jjj fff jjj fff jjj fff

jjj fff jjj fff jjj fff jjj fff jjj fff jjj fff jjj

Exercise 3

The next exercise mixes the letters typed by both hands. Type each line twice. Turn up an extra line space after each set of practice lines.

fjf fjf fjf fjf fjf fjf fjf fjf fjf fjf fjf fjf fjf

jfj jfj jfj jfj jfj jfj jfj jfj jfj jfj jfj jfj jfj

fjf jfj fjf jfj fjf jfj fjf jfj fjf fjf fjf fjf fjf

fjf jfj fjj jff fjj jff fjf jfj jjf ffj fff jjj fjf

8.4 Tips

Even if you are using a computer you should press the return key at the end of each line of exercises. The *wordwrap* function is used when typing continuous paragraphs of text, not individual lines.

Say each letter and space to yourself as you type, e.g., **j space j space j space.** Also try to develop a rhythm as you type, taking the same time to depress the letter and the space bar.

Right from the start you should read through your work and identify any errors. Do not attempt to correct the errors at this stage. Do not save the text if you are using a computer.

Always check your sitting position before starting to type:

1 Are your feet on the floor?
2 Is the height of your seat correct?
3 Are your hands poised over the home keys with your wrists straight?
4 Are your fingers slightly curved?
5 Are you using the correct typing action for your particular machine?

8.5 Proof-reading

It is useful to develop proof-reading skills on text typed by someone else and proof-reading tasks are provided throughout the book. The proof-reading exercise below has been printed twice. The first copy has been typed correctly, but the second copy contains typographical errors. Proof-read the second passage and see if you can identify all the errors. Your proof-reading skills may be checked against the key on p. 187.

```
When you learn to use a keyboard, you are training
your fingers to move away from the home keys in a
particular direction, and for a given distance.  It
is therefore important to return each finger to its
home key immediately after moving to strike another
key so that the next 'key reach' will be accurate.
```

```
When you learn to use a keyboard you are training
your fingers to to move away from the home keys in
a particular direction, and for  given distance.
it is therefore important to return each finger to
its home key immediately after moving to strike
another key so that the the next 'Key reach' will
be accurate.
```

Chapter 9

The Use of Keys d and k

Deletion of Text

Using a computer for typing allows easy and quick deletion of what has been typed. A single character, word, line, or a whole sentence may be deleted. Even paragraphs and pages of text may be deleted, virtually at the touch of a key. Documents may be eliminated completely from disk. This being so, the delete function must be used with great care, especially when deleting paragraphs, pages and documents. Systems which alert the typist by displaying a prompt on screen such as 'ARE YOU SURE' are better than those which just go ahead and delete text without a prompt. Remember to read your screen prompts every time you carry out a function.

9.1 Guidelines

Place your fingers over the home key row. The middle finger of the right hand is used to depress the letter **k** key and the middle finger of the left hand is used to depress the letter **d** key.

Manual typewriter
Take care not to move any other finger of either hand while the letter **d** or **k** key is being depressed. Pressure on more than one key at a time on a manual typewriter can cause the striking mechanism of the keys to become entangled. If this happens they will have to be released manually. Repeated entanglement can result in damage to the typing mechanism.

Computer
Take care not to move any other finger of either hand while the letter **d** or **k** key is being depressed. A slight pressure on any other key will result in additional letters being typed.

9.2 Exercises

Exercise 1

This exercise introduces you to two new letters **d** and **k**. Read the guidelines and practise the exercise, typing each line once.

Location Drills

dd dd dd dd dd dd dd dd dd dd dd dd dd dd dd dd
kk kk kk kk kk kk kk kk kk kk kk kk kk kk kk kk

dk dk dk dk dk dk dk dk dk dk dk dk dk dk dk dk
kd kd kd kd kd kd kd kd kd kd kd kd kd kd kd kd

dkd kdk dkk dkd kdd kdk dkk dkd kdk dkd kdk dkd

Exercise 2

The next exercise combines the typing of all four letters learnt so far. Type the exercise twice. Try to type this exercise without looking at your fingers. Keep your eyes on the copy as you type.

Location Drills

```
dk dj df kj kf fj fk fd jk jd dj fj dk fj df kj
jd fd fj jd kj dj jk fk dk kf df dk jf fd jf kd

fd jk df kj fd jk df kj fd jk df kj fd jk df kj

dkj kfd jkj fdk djf kdk jfd fkj dfd dkf fkd fjd
kjk jdk fjf dfd fkj jfd kdk djf fdk jkj kfd dkj
```

9.3 Proof-reading

The paragraph below has been printed twice. The first copy has been typed correctly, but the second copy contains typographical errors. Proof-read the second passage and see if you can identify all the errors. Your proof-reading skills may be checked against the key on p. 188.

```
In the early stages of keyboard training you shoul
not attempt to correct any errors you may make.
Your main aim at this stage is to learn the correc
key reaches.  If the key reach is accurate, then
the printed text will also be accurate.  If you
have struck the wrong key by mistake, correcting
the error on the page (or on the screen) is of
little benefit.  Direct your practice to learning
the correct key reaches so that you strike the
correct key with the appropriate finger.
```

```
In the early stages of keyboard training you shoul
not should not attempt to correct any errors you
may make.  You main aim at this stage is to learn
the correct key reaches.  If the key reach is
accurate then the printed text will be accurate.
If you have struck the wrong key by mistake, then
correcting the error on the page (or on the screen
is of little benefit.  Direct your practise to
learning   correct key reaches so that you strike
the correct key with with the appropriate finger.
```

Chapter 10

The Use of Keys s and l

Screen Aids

The best computer word processing programs are those which aid the typist by showing a prompt line on screen. This line may be at the top of the screen or at the bottom of the screen. A question may be displayed on the line, information may be displayed, it may offer guidance, or it may require action from the typist before the program will continue. It may also alert the typist to the fact that text will be lost if the present action is continued. Screen aids are very useful and the typist should keep glancing at the prompt line whenever carrying out word processing functions.

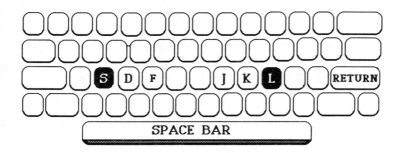

10.1 Guidelines

Press the letter **s** key with the third finger of the left hand and the letter **l** key with the third finger of the right hand. Look at the keyboard to identify the positions of the keys. When you feel confident that you know the location of the **s** and **l** keys, try to keep your eyes on the copy. Place your fingers on the home keys and type the exercise.

Remember to set single line spacing for all exercises, and a line length of 50 letter spaces. Always allow for a top margin whenever you use a new sheet of paper (see p. 25).

10.2 Exercises

Exercise 1 introduces the new letters s and l. Exercise 2 combines the new keys with those already learnt.

Type each line twice, leaving a clear line space between sets of practice lines.

Exercise 1

Location Drills

```
ss ll ss ll ss ll ss ll ss ll ss ll ss ll ss ll

sls lsl ssl lls sls lsl ssl lls sls sls lsl sls
```

Exercise 2

```
fjf jfj dkd kdk sls lsl fds jkl sls fjs jfl lsl

sld lds dfd jls sks dsk dfs lsd sll dls jdl sls

lkd sls kld dfl slf lfd fls skl slk kld skl lsl

lks ldl skd sds sfd lfs jkd lss kld jld fdl sls

sdf lkj fds jkl sdf lkj fds jkl sdf lkj fds lkj
```

10.3 Tips

Always proof-read your work while the paper is in the typewriter, or proof-read from screen on a computer. Do not correct any errors at this stage. You are trying to establish accurate key reaches at the moment. An incorrect letter printed on the paper shows that the key reach was not made correctly—correcting the error on the paper does not improve the accuracy of your key reaches. Try to identify the causes of any errors you may have made (see p. 35) and return to the appropriate chapter to carry out some remedial work.

10.4 Proof-reading

The passage below has been printed twice. The first copy has been typed correctly, but there are typographical errors in the second copy. Proof-read the passage and see if you can identify all the errors. Your proof-reading skills may be checked against the key on p. 188.

Many people insist that 'touch typists' should be able to type page after page of text without ever looking at the keyboard. Inexperienced typists therefore feel a sense of guilt if they steal a glance now and again at the keyboard to gain confidence. Obviously it is inefficient to look at the keyboard all the time, but research has shown that even the most experienced typists are constantly glancing at the keyboard – in much the same way that a driver is constantly glancing in the mirror without taking his or her attention from the road.

Many people insist that 'touch typists should be able to type page after page of text without ever looking at the keyboard Inexperienced typists therefore feel a sense of giult if they steal a glance now and then at the keyboard to gain confidence. Obviously it is inefficient to loook at the keyboard all the time, but research has shown that even the most experience typists are constantly glancing at the keyboard in much the same the same way that a driver is constantly glancing in the mirror without taking his attention from the road.

Chapter 11

The Use of Keys a and ;

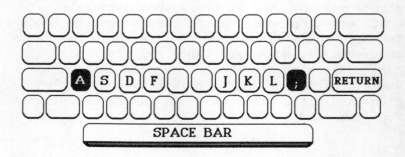

Page Breaks

The size of the paper used in a manual typewriter physically controls the size of the page. The length of a page when using a computer is set in different ways: (a) when setting margins, (b) after typing the document, or (c) the system does it automatically.

The end of the page is shown by a marker, such as a line of asterisks or spaced dashes across the screen, or by a mark in the left margin. These markers are known as *page breaks*. Those which are set automatically by the computer are known as *soft page breaks*, whereas those which are set by the typist are termed *hard page breaks*. Soft page breaks are adjusted automatically by the computer each time a document is 'paginated' (divided into pages), whereas hard page breaks have to be adjusted by a command from the typist.

11.1 Guidelines

Look at the keyboard and locate the letter **a** key and the **;** key. The letter **a** is at the left of the keyboard and the **;** at the right of the keyboard.

The little finger of the left hand is used to depress the letter **a** key and the little finger of the right hand is used to depress the **;** key.

Place your fingers over the home key row. You will probably find that you need to raise the other fingers of each hand slightly when striking the **a** and **;** keys. Always return them *immediately* to their home keys.

11.2 Exercises

This exercise introduces the letter **a** and the semi-colon (;). Type the location drill, following the fingering as described in the guidelines. When you feel that you know the location of these new letters, progress onto the words, which are designed to help consolidate the key reaches. Type each line twice.

Location Drills

```
aa aa ;; ;; aa ;; aa ;; aa ;; ;; aa aa ;; ;; aa
a; ;a aa ;; a; ;a aa ;; a; ;a aa ;; a; ;a aa ;a

aa; ;;a aa; ;;a aa; ;;a aa; ;;a aa; a;a ;a; a;;

asdf ;lkj asdf ;lkj asdf ;lkj a;fjsldk a;fjsldk
fdsa jkl; fdsa jkl; fdsa jkl; jf;alskd jf;alskd
```

Words

```
all add ask as; dad lad fad sad as; all ask dad

lass asks fads adds lads dads falls lass; asks;

all lads ask; as flasks fall; ask all sad lads;

sad all flasks fall; add all flasks; all falls;
```

11.3 Tips

Line spacing

Follow the general typing rules given below for all your work.

1   Remember to allow for top and bottom margins.
2   Set single line spacing for the exercises in each chapter.

3   Set a line length of 50 letter spaces.
4   Press the return key (or operate the carriage return lever) once at the end of each line.
5   Press the return key twice at the end of a section or paragraph, or wherever you require an additional line space.

11.4 Proof-reading

The passage below has been typed twice. The first copy has been typed correctly, but the second contains typographical errors. Proof-read the second passage and see if you can identify all the errors. Your proof-reading skills may be checked against the key on p. 188.

```
When you are using a word processor, the
word wrap facility takes care of line
endings automatically, and there is no
need for the operator to use the return
key when typing continuous paragraphs of
text.  However, it is necessary to use
the return key to insert a 'hard return'
at the end of: a heading, a paragraph, a
single line of text, each line of a
tabulated statement and wherever an extra
line space is required.
```

```
When you are using a wrod processor, the
wordwrap facility takes care of line
'endings automatically, and there is no
no need for the operator to use the return
key when typing continous paragraphs of
text.  However, it is necessary to use
the return to insert a 'hard return'
at the end of; a heading, a paragraph, a
single line of text, each line of a of a
tabulated statement and wher ever an extra
line space is required.
```

Chapter 12

The Use of Keys e and i

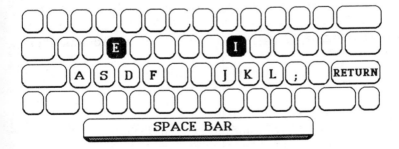

12.1 Guidelines

Now that you are confident about the location of the home keys, it is possible to start moving around the keyboard. The next two letters to be learnt are **e** and **i**. They are situated on the upper row of letter keys. Look at the keyboard and identify the new keys.

To strike the **e** key, move your left hand up one row of keys and to the left, keeping the fingers slightly curved. Press the letter **e** key with the middle finger of the left hand (the **d** finger), and immediately return all fingers to the home keys.

To strike the **i** key, move your right hand up one row of keys and to the left, keeping the fingers slightly curved. Press the letter **i** key with the middle finger of the right hand (the **k** finger), and immediately return all fingers to the home keys.

Always keep the fingers of the hand you are not using close to their home keys.

12.2 Exercises

Place your fingers over the home keys and practise the movements described in the guidelines without actually pressing the new keys.

Look at the keyboard while you practise moving the fingers from the home keys to the upper row of letter keys, with the middle finger of the left hand reaching to the letter **e** key and the middle finger of the right hand reaching to the letter **i** key.

Then try the same movements without looking at the keyboard. Remember to move one hand and return it to the home keys before moving the other hand. When you feel reasonably confident with the key reaches, practise the exercises. Type each line twice.

Location Drills

```
ed ed ed ed ik ik ik ik ed ik ed ik ed ed ik ik

ded kik ded kik ded kik ded ded kik ded kik dkd

edk edk ikd ikd ede iki ede iki edk ikd ded kik
```

Words
```
fed ill see fee did lee aid led kid lie ale eel

feed sill seal disk seed lead feel leaf sail is
silk jade dial file safe like disk idle lies as

disks false skills ladle sidle fiddle killed is
```

12.3 Tips
Screen sizes

The screens of visual display units come in various shapes and sizes. Their size is not measured in inches or centimetres but by the amount of text which can be displayed on the screen. The width is given in column width, that is, the number of letters which can be displayed across the screen. The most common size is 80 columns which is equivalent to the amount of text that can fit on a piece of A4 paper placed portrait-wise in a manual typewriter. However, screens can range in width from 40 columns to 120 columns.

The height of the screen is given in terms of the number of lines of text that can be displayed. The most general size is around 25 lines, but they can range from around 20 lines up to 60 lines. After allowing for margins, about 60 or so lines of text can be typed on A4 paper placed portrait-wise in a manual typewriter.

Little can be done about selecting a manual typewriter with regard to the amount of text that can be typed, apart from choice of pitch size and the length of the carriage. Some thought should be given to screen size when selecting a computer, especially if it is to be put to use as a word processor.

12.4 Proof-reading

The following passage has been printed twice. The first copy has been typed correctly, but the second copy contains typographical errors. Proof-read the second passage and see if you can identify all the errors. Your proof-reading skills may be checked against the key on p. 189.

```
If you use a word processor, it is in your
own interest to take care of your floppy
disks.  Keep them away from sources of
heat (such as radiators or sunny window
sills), and from sources of magnetic
radiation (such as the system itself or
even the telephone).  When not in use,
disks should be stored in a rigid box.
```

```
If you use a wordprocessor, it is in you
own interests to take care of your floppy
disks.Keep them away from sources of heat
heat such as radiators or sunny window
sills), and from sources of magnetic
radiation (such as the System itself or
even the telephone).  When not in use
disks should be stored in a rigid case.
```

Chapter 13

The Use of Keys r and t

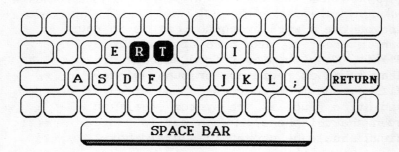

Scrolling

The screen of the VDU is looked upon as a window for viewing text which has been input into the computer. Text which is too long or too wide to show on the screen may be moved up, down and across the screen to show the additional text. This movement is known as *vertical scrolling* when moving text up or down the screen, and *horizontal scrolling* when moving to left or right. Smooth scrolling line by line or letter by letter is essential for ease of reading and understanding.

13.1 Guidelines

Typing is not a matter of alternately depressing one letter with a finger of the left hand and another with a finger of the right hand. One hand alone may be involved in typing a word. The first exercise in this chapter, using the new letters **r** and **t**, includes practice in typing words involving the use of one hand only.

Place both hands over the home keys, and look at the keyboard while learning the key reaches to help you gain confidence and make accurate finger movements.

To depress the letter **r** key, move all the fingers of the left hand upwards and to the left, keeping the fingers slightly curved. Depress the letter **r** key with the index finger of the left hand (the **f** finger) and immediately return the fingers to the home keys. While you are using your left hand, remember to keep the fingers of the right hand hovering over their home keys.

To depress the letter **t** key, move all the fingers of the left hand upwards and to the *right,* keeping the fingers slightly curved. Depress the letter **t** key with the index finger of the left hand (the **f** finger) and immediately return the fingers to the home keys. While you are using your left hand, remember to keep the fingers of the right hand hovering over their home keys.

At the learning stage it is very important that you *always* return your fingers to the home keys between key reaches, even when adjacent keys such as **r** and **t** are being struck. You are training your fingers to make key reaches from the home keys, not from one key to another.

13.2 Exercises

Practise the movements described in the guidelines without actually typing the letters, looking at the keyboard to ensure that you make confident key reaches. Once you feel reasonably confident with your finger movements and your ability to locate the new letters without looking, type the location drills and words provided in the exercises. Type each line at least twice.

Location Drills

rf rf rf rf rf rf rf rf rf rf rf rf rf rf rf rf
tf tf tf tf tf tf tf tf tf tf tf tf tf tf tf tf

frf ftf frf ftf frf ftf frf ftf frf ftf frf ftf
rfr tft rfr tft rfr tft rfr tft rfr tfr rfr tft

dr dr dt dt st sr ar at fr ra ta ts kr lt rk rl

Words

art set rat set eat tea art sat are sit eat tea

seat feet dart date read free last lead real at

fret dirt rail late east data jest tail seat it

steak start treat trade later steel risks trial

```
it is a desk; details are free; as a free trial
all address lists are at risk; take a free disk

sell a steel disk safe later; trade is at risk;
take a disk; test it; read all data; erase data

a street trader sat at a free seat; sit at tea;
all trial disks are treated; test a trial disk;
```

13.3 Tips

Incorrect lighting can be very tiring to your eyes. Always check that the light is adjusted correctly for you before starting a typing session. Remember, too much light directed on the pages of this book or on the VDU screen may cause headaches, whilst too little light may lead to eye strain.

If possible, use a copyholder so that your copy material is placed in the most suitable position, preferably at eye level.

13.4 Proof-reading

The passage below has been printed twice. The first passage has been typed correctly, but the second passage contains typographical errors. Proof-read the second passage and see if you can identify all the errors. Your proof-reading skills may be checked against the key on p. 189.

```
You should by now have developed the habit
of proofreading your work.  If you have made
any errors, try to identify the causes of
these errors.  In many cases they will be
caused by incorrect key reaches.  Practise
the faulty key reaches, looking at your
fingers to ensure that your hand movement
is correct and the reach confidently made.

You should have developed the habit by now
of proofreading your work.  If you have made
errors, try to identify the causes of these
these errors.  In many cases they will be
caused by in correct key reaches.  Practice
the faulty key reaches looking at your
fingers to ensure that your hand movements
are correct and the reach confidently made
```

Chapter 14

The Use of Keys g and h

Typing Speed

Typing speed may be slower on a manual keyboard than on an electronic one. This is because it takes more effort to depress the keys on a manual keyboard and also the typing mechanism responds more slowly. However, an average typist can reach speeds of 50-60 words per minute on a manual typewriter and some very experienced ones can reach speeds of up to 125 words per minute. The secret lies in gaining complete mastery of the keyboard and then using minimum eye movement from text to keyboard—in other words, keeping your eyes on the copy as much as possible.

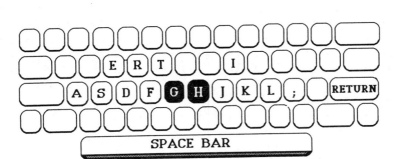

14.1 Guidelines

The letters **g** and **h** complete the home key row. The letter **g** key is depressed with the index finger of the left hand (the **f** finger) and the letter **h** key is depressed with the index finger of the right hand (the **j** finger). Look at the keyboard until you can make the key reaches confidently. Place your fingers over the home keys.

73

To strike the **g** key, move all the fingers of your left hand across to the right a little. Depress the **g** key and *immediately* return all your fingers to the home keys.

To strike the **h** key, move all the fingers of your right hand across to the left a little. Depress the **h** key and *immediately* return all your fingers to the home keys.

14.2 Exercises

Practise the key reaches without actually typing the letters. Then type the location drills. When you feel competent, move on to the words. Type each line at least twice.

Location Drills

```
fg jh fg jh fg jh gf hj gf hj fg jh fg jh gf hj
fg fg jh jh dg dg kh kh sg sg lg lf kg kg sh sh

fgf jhj fgf jhj fgf jhj fgf jhj fgf jhj fgf jhj
lih gre sgh hil thi agd ght hig lgs sha igh gha

asdfgfa ;lkjhj; asdfgfa ;lkjhj; asdfgfa ;lkjhj;
```

Words

```
the has get tag dig his her leg gas hit fig lag

high that this sight thigh light eight lighter;
great three fight height freight fighter right;

his test flight is late at the gate;
get that lighter; the data is right;


get all the disks; hire a freighter;
it is a great sale; get these right;
```

14.3 Tips

Keep the room in which you are typing well ventilated. This does not mean that the door or window must be open at all times, but a regular change of air is necessary. A feeling of drowsiness, especially after lunch, is a sure sign of a stuffy atmosphere. Do something about it before you lose your concentration. Loss of concentration may be one cause of typing errors.

14.4 Proof-reading

The following passage below has been printed twice. The first copy has been typed correctly, but the second copy contains typographical errors. Proof-read the second passage and see if you can identify all the errors. Your proof-reading skills may be checked against the key on p. 189.

Listing Paper

A computer program is written and then input
into the computer. What has been input can
be printed and this printed form is known as
a program listing. The program listing,
because it is usually very long, is printed
on continuous stationery which has bands of
fine lines and open spaces evenly distributed
throughout the length of the paper. This has
led to this type of continuous stationery
being termed listing paper.

Listing Paper

a computer programme is written and then put
into the computer What has beeen input can
be printed nad this printed from is known as
a program listing. The program listng
because it is usually very long, is printed
on contenuous stationary which has bands of
of fine lines and open spaces evenly
destributed thrughout the length of the paper
This has led to this type of continuus
stationery being termed listing paper.

Chapter 15

The Use of Keys u and o

Typing Speed and Production Rate

A good typist can type both accurately and speedily. When you produce a typewritten document, the speed at which you work includes not only the time taken for the typing but also the time involved in preparation of your work, putting the paper in the machine, proof-reading and—when you have completed the keyboard stage—making any corrections needed. The total time taken is your 'production rate', and this is a more meaningful measure of your keyboarding skills than a straightforward measurement of copy-typing speed.

When assessing a person's production rate, both typing speed and accuracy are important factors. A person with a high typing speed may be very inaccurate, whilst a slow typist may be very accurate. However, neither of these extremes is desirable, and you should aim to develop a good typing speed together with a consistently high level of accuracy.

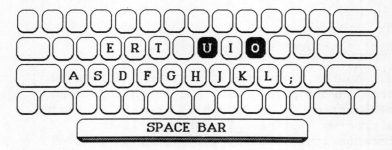

15.1 Guidelines

The next letters are **u** and **o**. These keys are located on the right half of the top row of the letter keys, and both are operated with fingers of the right hand.

To strike the letter **u** key, move all the fingers of the right hand upwards and slightly to the left. Use the index finger (the **j** finger) to strike the letter **u** and *immediately* return all fingers to the home row. To strike the letter **o** key, move all the fingers of the right hand upwards and slightly to the left. Use the third finger (the **k** finger) to strike the letter **o** and *immediately* return all fingers to the home row.

Remember that in the learning stages it is important to start all key reaches from the home row, and to return all fingers to the home row once a key has been struck. If you need to type the letter **o** twice, as in the word *too,* you should return your fingers to the home row each time you strike the letter. Even if you are typing adjacent keys such as **r** and **t**, as in the word *cart,* you should return your fingers to the home keys after typing each letter.

15.2 Exercises

Look at the keyboard and practise the movements described in the guidelines without actually striking the letters. Keep the fingers of the left hand resting on the home keys while using the right hand. When you feel that you can locate the keys confidently without looking, practise the location drills, followed by the word drills. Type each line twice.

Location Drills

```
lo lo lo lo lo lo lo lo lo lo lo lo lo lo lo lo
ju ju ju ju ju ju ju ju ju ju ju ju ju ju ju ju

lol juj lol juj lol juj lol juj lol juj lol juj
lol sol juk luk lou sou jui udo flo olo uso otd

asdfgfa ;lkjhj; asdf ;lkj gfgf hjhj asdfg ;lkjh
ded kik frf juj ftf lol ded kik frf juj ftf lol
```

Words

```
hut hot out oak rug hug log rut oil dug dot lot;

just true folk dust sold look lost took good go;

four store folio older route short trusts tough;
tougher sorter through through thorough outright
```

```
he taught the lad to store all these older disks
take the folios to the storage safe at the house
the author sorted through all the guides for her

our load of tough solids is routed through to us
our sales staff sold out of all these good disks


just store those three others; go to the stores;

order this folio through their sales order staff

he should get the stores order together at eight
```

15.3 Tips

Typing speed

Typing speed is stated in words per minute. It is calculated very simply. A typing 'word' is considered to be five keystrokes long, i.e., the striking of any type of key five times, including commas, full stops, spaces and carriage returns.

Speed development passages have been prepared to help you increase your typing speed, and you should measure your speed at regular intervals. At the early stages you should type for one minute and see how much of the passage you can type. You can later try testing your speed for two, three or four minutes.

Read off the number of words at the end of each complete line typed; if you have typed part of a line, the numbers below the passage indicate the number of words you have typed on the unfinished line. Add these numbers together; if you have typed for one minute, that figure gives your typing speed. Ignore any typing errors when calculating your typing speed. If you type for two minutes, divide the number of words by two.

At this stage your speed will probably be around eight to ten words a minute, and you should aim to reach at least twenty to twenty-five words a minute by the time you complete this book.

15.4 Proof-reading

The following passage has been printed twice. The first copy has been typed correctly but the second copy contains typographical errors.

Proof-read the second passage and see if you can identify all the errors.
Your proof-reading skills may be checked against the key on p. 190.

The typeface of manual typewriters, golf ball type
elements and printwheels becomes 'dirty' through a
build-up of ink from continuously striking the print
ribbon. If this is allowed to accumulate, the
centre of letters such as a, p, b, and e will become
blocked. It is good practice to clean the typeface
at regular intervals using the appropriate method.

The type face of manual typwriters, golf ball type
elements and printwheeels becomes 'dirty' through a
build up of ink from continuosly strikeing the rpint
ribbon If this is allowed to accumilate the
centre of leters such as a, p, b and e become
blocked. It is good practice to clean the typeface
at regular intevals using the appropriate method.

15.5 Speed Development

The speed development exercises are designed to help you improve
your typing skills and to assess your development. Your aim should be
to increase your typing speed without making too many typing errors.

Type the passage once at a speed you find comfortable. Copy the
passage line for line, but do not type the numbers. Repeat the passage
at a slightly faster rate. If you wish, you may try it a third time at a faster
rate again, but three attempts are all you should make at any one
sitting.

If you are inaccurate, analyse your typewritten work to identify the
type of error and the remedial work you need to carry out. If all your
errors are associated with a particular letter, return to the chapter
dealing with that letter. Practise the key reaches and the exercises until
you feel confident that you have mastered that reach. Erratic errors,
various letters sometimes typed correctly and other times not, may be
a sign that you are trying to type too fast. Slow down a little and
remember to say each letter, space and carriage return as you type.

The speed development exercises have been marked to help you
calculate your typing speed and they may be used for this purpose. If
you wish to test the speed at which you type, type at a rate you find
comfortable and reasonably accurate. To calculate your speed, follow
the instructions given in **15.3**, the 'Tips' section.

Speed development

Type for one minute. Do not type the numbers; these are printed to indicate the number of words typed.

Wor

```
he tried out these disks first; the girls fed all      1
the data to his disks; this is their eighth sheet      2
of data so tell the girls to rest; it is too late      3

    1     2     3     4     5     6     7     8     9    10
```

Chapter 16
The Use of Left Shift, Full Stop and Right Shift

Introduction

This chapter introduces capital letters and the full stop, and from now on most of the exercises will take the form of complete sentences.

When the first letter of a word is a capital letter it is known as an 'initial capital' or 'initial cap'. Initial capitals are typed by depressing the shift key and holding it down while the letter is typed. Once the letter has been typed, the shift key is released.

In handwriting we leave a space between a full stop and the start of the next sentence. However there is no 'rule' which says how wide that space should be. In typewriting the space is measured in letter spaces. In general, the following guidelines apply, and you should follow these as you progress through the book.

1   Every sentence starts with a capital letter (initial cap).
2   A comma (,), colon (:), semi-colon (;) or full-stop (.) is typed close up to the word or letter to which it is related in a sentence.
3   A single letter space is left after a comma, colon, or semi-colon.
4   Two letter spaces are left after a full stop.

16.1 Guidelines

The shift keys are located at the left and right of the bottom row of the letter keys. The shift keys are depressed with the little finger of each hand. When typing a letter with the right hand, the left shift key is used. The right shift key is depressed when the left hand is typing a capital letter.

No sentence is complete until it ends with a full stop. The full stop is found on the right hand side of the bottom row of keys. Strike the full stop by moving the fingers of the right hand downwards and to the right, keeping all the fingers slightly curved. Use the third finger of the right hand (the l finger) to strike the full stop key.

16.2 Exercises

Look at the keyboard to identify the positions of the two shift keys and the full stop key. Position your fingers over the home keys. Move your right hand downwards and to the right so that the little finger rests on the shift key, keeping all the other fingers slightly curved. Then return your fingers to the home keys. Practise the movement until you can locate the right shift key without looking.

Move the left hand downwards and to the left so that the little finger rests on the left shift key, keeping the other fingers slightly curved. Then return your fingers to the home keys. Practise the movement until you can locate the left shift key without looking. Repeat both movements, this time depressing the shift key. Type the first row of the location drill.

Once you feel that you have mastered the use of the shift key, practise the full stop. Look at the keyboard until you develop a confident key reach movement. Move your right hand down and slightly to the right. Strike the full stop key with the third finger of the right hand (the l finger), and *immediately* return all fingers to the home row. Practise locating the full stop key until you can locate the key with ease. Then type the second row of the location drill, followed by the remaining exercises. Type each line twice.

Exercise 1
Location Drills

Dd Ll Gf Hj Ff Jj Ss Ll Kk So Le Do Kr Go He Je

Frf Juj Ded Kik Ftf Lol Fgf Jhj Ded Fds Jkl Asd

l.l l.l l.l l.l l.l l.l l.l l.l l.l l.l l.l l.l

la. li. lo. le. ls. lk. ld. lj. lf. lr. lt. lu.

Words

Go. Do. Is. She. To. It. So. Are. Hers.
Just. Fought. Disk. Goal. Kit. List. Joe.

Details. Serial. Thorough. Guilded. Sorter.
Auditor. Guests. •Truthful. House. Fortress.

Sentences

Ask Juliette Dee to sit here at the Sales Desk.
Kate is four feet tall. Get her a higher seat.
Ask Arthur or Stuart to raise the seat for her.

Load that data file. Edit these address lists.
Do it like this. Go through all the old files.
Delete the outdated data. Delete all the data.
Test these hard disk utilities. They are good.
Do store the edited disks. Log off after that.

Exercise 2

This exercise is designed to cover all the letters learnt so far. Type each paragraph twice.

I realise that the disk looks old; just look at the state of it. Take it out of use. Get a fresh disk out of the store for future use. Use good disks so that data is safeguarded.

To safeguard the disks staff are asked to eat their food outside. Staff should eat at their rest house sited just off Restford Street to the right of Gate Eight or at the other rest house at Eastleigh Road.

16.3 Proof-reading

The following passage has been printed twice. The first copy has been typed correctly, but the second copy contains typographical errors.

Proof-read the second passage and see if you can identify all the errors. Your proof-reading skills may be checked against the key on p. 190.

Office Security

Computers can offer great flexibility in the preparation of documents. They may be edited a number of times quite easily. However, some documents may be private and confidential and what happens to the discarded drafts of the document could be vitally important to the business. For this reason many businesses use paper shredders in the office. All unwanted paperwork, which would normally go into a waste paper basket, is put through the shredder.

Officer Security

Computers can offer great flexability in the preparation of documents. They may be edited a number of times quiet easily. However, some doucments may be private and confidentail and what happens to the the descarded drafts of the document could be vitaly important to the bussiness. For this reason many businessses use paper shredders in in the office. All unwanted paperwrok which would normally go into a wast paper baskit, is put thorugh the shredder.

16.4 Speed Development

Wor

It is all right for her to use these disks so ask   1
her to load this data for the order. Look at the   2
utilities disks. See if the old data is deleted.   3

    1   2   3   4   5   6   7   8   9   10

Chapter 17

The Use of Keys y and p

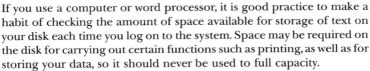

Disk Space

If you use a computer or word processor, it is good practice to make a habit of checking the amount of space available for storage of text on your disk each time you log on to the system. Space may be required on the disk for carrying out certain functions such as printing, as well as for storing your data, so it should never be used to full capacity.

It is usual to leave around 25 pages clear on the disk. The amount of space available may be given in terms of pages or as KBytes. Refer to your user manual to find out how to check on the space available on your disk. Remember to make a habit of checking the available disk space whenever you log on to the system.

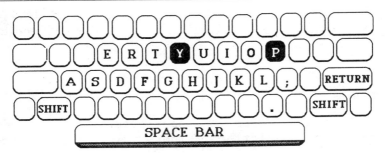

17.1 Guidelines

The letter **y** and **p** keys are situated on the top row of letter keys. They are both depressed by the fingers of the right hand.

To strike the letter **y** key, move all the fingers of the right hand upwards and slightly to the left. Usé the index finger (the **j** finger) to strike the letter **y**, and *immediately* return all fingers to the home row.

To strike the letter **p** key, move all the fingers of the right hand

86 *The Use of Keys y and p*

upwards and slightly to the left. Use the little finger (the **;** finger) to
strike the letter **p**, and *immediately* return all fingers to the home row.

17.2 Exercises

Look at the keyboard and practise reaching for these letters until you
can locate the keys with confidence. Keep the fingers of the left hand
resting over the home keys while using the right hand. Practise the key
reaches again without looking at the keyboard.

When you feel ready, practise the location drills, words and
sentences. Type each line twice.

Location Drills

```
;p ;p ;p ;p jy jy jy jy sp dy s; d; ly lp fy fp ap
;p; jyj ;p; ftf ;p; frf ;p; ded ;p; jyj kik lol ;p
lp; lop juy hyj lyj phl dyk jpl ph; gp; dy; spa p;
```

Words

```
key pay fly pad jay tap you put guy ply yes alp up
day pit say pot yet top lay pet dry pie try joy ay
```

```
your page stay poor year past keys push trap play;
press today phase happy repay youth apply replies;
```

```
yearly prepare possess hardly steady phrase ports;
profit Yorkshire property yesterday Poole plotter;
```

Sentences

```
Get the adaptor plug for the plotter; put it here.
Please use the plotter if there is a paper supply.
```

```
Ask Pat Pyler to put the paper through the hopper.
The other operators usually use up the hard disks.
```

```
There are fifty or so floppy disks stored up here.
You should order further supplies of floppy disks.
```

```
Key this data to the spreadsheet files for safety.
Perhaps you should keep these files free of error.
```

17.3 Tips

Remember to check your sitting position each time you sit at your workstation. If you constantly change your position as you type, you are also changing the distance and the direction in which your fingers should move, and this results in errors. The points to remember are:

1 Are your feet on the floor?
2 Is the height of your seat correct? Use a cushion to raise yourself if the seat cannot be adjusted.
3 Are your hands poised over the home keys with your wrists straight? You will find this position helps to increase your typing speed. If the palms of your hands rest on the keyboard while you type, your speed is bound to be affected.
4 Are you concentrating on the typing action required for your particular machine? If you use an electronic typewriter or computer keyboard, remember to use a very light touch.

17.4 Proof-reading

The following passage has been printed twice. The first copy has been typed correctly but the second copy contains typographical errors. Proof-read the second passage and see if you can identify all the errors. Your proof-reading skills may be checked against the key on p. 190.

Fire Precautions

Wherever there is electricity and electrical
equipment in use there is the potential danger of
fire resulting from an electrical fault. For this
reason every home and business should have a fire
extinguisher. Special extinguishers which do not
conduct electricity must be used. Those containing
bromochlorodifluormethane are said to be efficient
in fighting fires caused through electrical faults.

Fire Precuations

Wherever their is electricity and electical
eqiupment in use there is the potential danger off
fire resulting from an electrical fautl. For this
reason evry home and buisiness should have a fire
extinguisher Special extinguishers which do not
conducct electricity must be used. These
containaining bromochlordiflourmethane are said to
be efficient fighting fires caused through
electrical faults

17.5 Speed Development

Wor

Please look up the rates for posting the letter to   1
Italy. You agreed to post the floppy disks off to   2
the people at Pisa. They are all ready to go out.   3

    1   2   3   4   5   6   7   8   9   10

Chapter 18

The Use of Keys c and n

Text Editing

The correction of typing errors, modification of the structure of a sentence or paragraph, amendments and the addition or deletion of words is known as editing. If you use a typewriter, any amendments necessary as a result of editing changes mean that you must re-type the whole document.

If you use a computer or word processor, text that has been saved to disk can be recalled to the screen. Editing changes can then be made quite simply through the use of various editing functions such as 'insert' and 'delete', and the revised version printed out. Refer to your user manual to check on the various editing facilities available on your system.

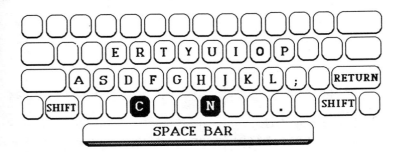

18.1 Guidelines

It is now time to learn some of the letters on the bottom row of keys. Look at the keyboard and identify the positions of the letter **c** and **n** keys. Identify their positions in relation to the home keys.

89

The letter **c** key is depressed with the middle finger of the left hand (the **d** finger). The letter **n** key is depressed with the index finger of the right hand (the **j** finger).

Look at the keyboard and place the fingers of both hands over the home keys. Move the right hand downwards and to the left, strike the letter **n** key with the index finger of the right hand and *immediately* return all fingers to the home keys.

Move the left hand downwards and to the right, strike the letter **c** key with the middle finger of the left hand and *immediately* return all fingers to the home keys.

18.2 Exercises

Look at the keyboard and practise the key reaches described in the guidelines without actually striking the keys. When you have gained confidence in locating the new keys, practise the key reaches without looking. When you feel confident about the positions of the **c** and **n** keys, practise the location drills and word exercises. Type each line twice.

Location Drills

```
jn jn jn jn dc dc dc dc an lc nj cd cl na jn dc cn
dcd jnj dcd jnj dcd jnj ded dcd juj dedcd jujnj nc

frf juj ded kik lol dcd ;p; jnj dcd kjn dcf pln sc
ftf juj ded dcd kik frf jnj juj jyj ;p; dcd jnj ck
```

Words

```
no in an on fan end can cat son cot ton act facts;

case plan node thin copy neck unit card jack face;
cost drain panic night crane screen access listing

secure special graphic analogue necessary acoustic
contract joystick processing interface negotiation
```

Sentences

Just take a glance at the central processing unit.
Use the special entry keys to log on to this unit.

The graphics application packages are in the safe.
Access this stock record and edit it if necessary.

Display the graphics chart on the coloured screen.
It is necessary to check on the printer interface.

Link the printer into the central processing unit.
Please insert the stationery into the hopper feed.

Unfortunately he thinks this printer is too noisy.
Reduce the noise. Enclose it in an acoustic hood.
Keep the lid securely closed until it has printed.

18.3 Tips

As you gain experience with keyboarding, you will find that you are generally aware of any errors you may make. If you use a computer or a word processor you may wish to start using the backspace delete key to correct an error immediately you have made it by deleting the incorrect letter and typing in the correct letter. This is also possible if you use an electric or electronic typewriter fitted with a correction ribbon.

If you use a manual typewriter, you should not backspace and type in the correct letter, as this simply results in two letters being printed in the same space. This is known as 'overtyping'.

However, you should remember that the most important thing at this stage in your development of keyboarding skills is to ensure that you make the correct key reaches. If you do this the number of errors you make will be reduced. If you are unsure about any particular key reach, spend a few minutes on revision and practice of location drills from the appropriate chapter.

18.4 Proof-reading

 The passage below has been printed twice. The first copy has been typed correctly, but there are typographical errors in the second copy. Proof-read the second passage and see if you can identify all the errors. Your proof-reading skills may be checked against the key on p. 191.

Envelopes Galore

Everyone needs envelopes at some time, whether for the home, sports club, educational establishment or for business. We have the right envelope for every occasion, from perfumed for the romantic, to self-adhesive for the overworked.

Why not advertise your business by having your company logo and address printed on the envelope? Send for details of our range of envelopes today.

Envelops Galore

Everyone needs envelopes at some time, weather for the home, Sports Club, educatoinal edstablishment or business. We have the right envelop for each ocasion, from perfumed for the romantic, to self-adhesive for the overworked.
Why not advertise your business by having your Company Logo and addresss printed on the envelope.
Send for detials of our range of envelopes today.

18.5 Speed Development

Wor

Please check to see if the engineer is calling in   ]
to service the central processing unit. There is   2
no point in logging on until after he has checked   3
it out and found the source of the strange noise.   4

    1   2   3   4   5   6   7   8   9   10

Chapter 19

The Use of Keys v and m

What makes a good keyboard operator?

A good typist or keyboard operator needs to be fast, accurate and efficient. However, there are a number of other important aspects to be considered. You need to have a reasonable command of English grammar, its usage, punctuation, vocabulary and of course spelling ability. If you know that your spelling is not as good as it should be, then you should make a habit of using a dictionary to check on spellings.

If you use a computer or word processor, your system may have a spelling check facility which will be of some assistance, though it may contain a limited number of words in its memory. You also need self-discipline and organisational ability. You will need to organise your day's work, including filing paper documents, and perhaps cope with continuous interruptions while maintaining concentration on the job in hand.

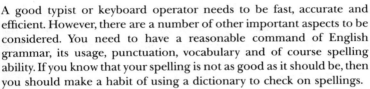

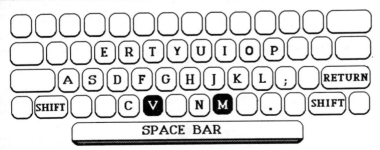

19.1 Guidelines

The next letters to be learnt on the bottom row of keys are **v** and **m**. The letter **v** key is depressed with the index finger of the left hand (the **f** finger). The letter **m** key is depressed with the index finger of the right

93

hand (the **j** finger). Look at the keyboard to identify the positions of the new keys, and to help you gain confidence with the new key reaches.

To strike the letter **v** key, place the fingers over the home keys and move the left hand downwards and slightly to the right. Strike the **v** key with the index finger and *immediately* return all the fingers to the home keys.

To strike the letter **m** key, move the right hand downwards and slightly to the right. Strike the letter **m** key and *immediately* return all the fingers to the home keys.

19.2 Exercises

Look at the keyboard and practise the new key reaches as described in the guidelines until you can locate the keys with confidence. Start by practising the movements without actually striking the keys. When you have gained confidence with the key reaches, practise locating the letters without looking at your hands.

Practise the location drills, words and sentences. Type each line twice.

Location Drills

```
jm jm jm jm fv fv fv fv sm kv dm lc md cl vp am mp

jmj fvf jmj fvf jmj fvf jmj fvf jmj fvf jmj fvf vm
ftf jyj fgf jhj frf juj fvf jmj ftf jyj fvf jmj mv

ded kik dcd ded dcd jnj frf juj ded kik fgf jhj mv
lol fmj ;p; dmj jmk jmk dfv sav fiv mlk lov lim fv
```

Words

```
me my mine gone gave have make came avoid leave my
save milk have made five mark menu move calm even;

lever media claim avoid visual curved video mouse;

device memory formed cover program middle magnetic
computer information manage campaign master divide
```

Sentences

The electronic calculator is a very simple form of
computer that can make very rapid calculations.

It is interesting to note that the memory of these
small machines is much larger than the memory of
the original computers of forty years ago that
filled a large room.

Perhaps you may find this a very useful item of
information if you are playing trivial pursuit
games that test your memory.

There are three major forms of computer; the large
mainframe computer, the minicomputer and the small
microcomputer that is sometimes called a personal
computer.

19.3 Tips

Typing can be quite tiring to your hands and arms in the early stages of
learning to type. Fatigue can be minimised by sitting properly at your
keyboard, of course. However, it is also important to keep your
practice sessions short and to have frequent rest periods, even if they
last for only a minute or two.

Research has shown that the best way to acquire a skill is to have
short practice periods at frequent, regular intervals. You will learn
more quickly if you spend half an hour at the keyboard twice a day on
each day of the week than if you practise for three or four hours on a
single day.

19.4 Proof-reading

The following passage has been printed twice. The first copy has been
typed correctly but the second copy contains typographical errors.
Proof-read the second passage and see if you can identify all the errors.
Your proof-reading skills may be checked against the key on p. 191.

SEARCH AND REPLACE

The search and replace function offered by most
computers is extremely useful. If a particular
word is spelt incorrectly throughout a document,
you can instruct the system to find all instances
of the word and replace them with the correct
spelling. Alternatively, you may wish to replace a
word such as 'automobile' with the word 'car'
throughout the document, or to replace an
abbreviation such as VDU with the full wording.

SEARCH OR REPLACE

The search and replace facility offered by most
computers is extremely useful. If a particularly
word is spelt incorrectly through out a document,
you can instruct the system to find all instances
of the word and to replace them with the correct
spelling. alternatively, you may wish to replace
word such as 'automobile' with the word 'car'
throughout the document, to or replace an
an abbreviation such as vdu with the full word.

19.5 Speed Development

Wc

We must improve our corporate sales of the memory
devices and at the same time maintain a very high
profile in the main street with individual sales.
It is vital to increase our market share greatly.

1   2   3   4   5   6   7   8   9   10

Chapter 20

The Use of Keys w and b

The Dictionary

Some word processor programs have a built-in dictionary—a program consisting of a certain number of words which have been spelt correctly. When the typist instructs the computer to carry out a spelling check, every word in the text of a document is checked against the words in the dictionary.

Words that are incorrectly spelt are highlighted or indicated in some way. Any words that are not in the dictionary are also indicated as being incorrectly spelt, simply because the computer does not recognise them. The dictionary needs to be very large, in the region of 180,000 words, if it is to be really useful.

Some spelling-check programs permit the typist to add words to the dictionary, or to compile personal sub-dictionaries containing words associated with a particular type of business. One disadvantage is that dictionaries do not identify grammatical errors such as 'there' for 'their' or 'where' for 'were', because these words are spelt correctly even if they are not used properly. Computer dictionaries can be a help with proof-reading but they do have some limitations.

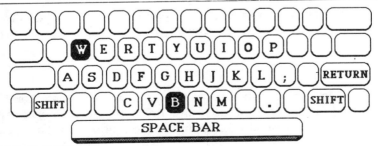

20.1 Guidelines

The letter **w**, which is on the top row of letter keys, towards the left, is struck with the third finger of the left hand (the **s** finger). The letter **b** which is in the middle of the bottom row of letter keys, is struck with the index finger of the left hand (the **f** finger). Look at the keyboard to identify the positions of the new keys. Place your fingers over the home keys.

To depress the **w** key, move your left hand upwards and to the left, keeping the fingers slightly curved. Strike the letter **w** key with the third finger of the left hand and *immediately* return all the fingers to the home keys.

To depress the **b** key, move your left hand downwards and to the right, keeping the fingers slightly curved. Strike the letter **b** key with the index finger of the left hand and *immediately* return all the fingers to the home keys.

Remember to keep the fingers of the right hand over the home keys while you are using your left hand.

20.2 Exercises

Look at the keyboard and practise the new key reaches as described in the guidelines until you can locate the keys confidently without looking at the keyboard. Start by practising the movements without actually striking the keys. When you feel confident that you can locate the new letters, practise the key reaches without looking at your hands.

Practise the location drills and the word and sentence exercise material. Type each line twice.

Location Drills

```
sw sw sw sw fb fb fb fb jw jw lb lb ws bf sw bk fb
sws lol ded kik frf juj ftf jyj asdfgfa ;lkjhj; wb

sws lol l.1 ded dcd kik sws frf fbf juj jmj sws fv
sws swd blk jmb jlb fdw bkl wds bks lws obj stw ib
```

Words

```
was buy saw bin job new bit ban raw win byte lower
bar with boot work baud went been ware base blower
were watch below wheel board which about batch few

keyboard brown switch window bought binary bankers
networking broken twelve viewdata twenty benchmark
```

Sentences

Take a batch of work to the new computer workshop.
The keyboard of the new word processor was broken.

Bring a batch of data back and we will work on it.
We bought new switches and twenty big base boards.

The word bit is really an abbreviation formed from
the words binary digit. It takes the first letter
of the word binary and the last two letters of the
word digit. A byte consists of eight bits.

A wide area network is a communications system for
sending messages electronically from one computer
to another over long distances. This method of
communication is often called electronic mailing.

20.3 Tips

For greatest efficiency, the text you are copying should be at eye level.
The most convenient method of ensuring that the copy is in this
position is to use a copy holder. Most copy holders have a line finder
which can be moved down the page of text one line at a time, so that
the line of text to be typed is easily identified.

The line finder may be moved down manually, but the more
sophisticated copy holders have an electrically-operated foot control
pedal for 'hands free' operation. Typing speed is said to increase if a
copy holder is used because the typist is not continually having to
identify the line to be typed. The use of a copy holder is also said to
reduce strain and fatigue.

20.4 Proof-reading

The following passage has been printed twice. The first copy has been
typed correctly but the second copy contains typographical errors.
Proof-read the second passage and see if you can identify all the errors.
Your proof-reading skills may be checked against the key on p. 192.

Copies of Documents

The traditional way of obtaining additional copies
of a document is to make carbon copies at the time
cf typing the original. This can be very time-
consuming, depending on the accuracy of the
typist, because typing errors have to be corrected
on each carbon copy. In many organisations carbon
copies are no longer used, and copies are made on
the photocopier.

Copys of Documents

The traditional way of obtining additional copies
of a document isto make copies at the time of
typing the orginal. This could be very time
consuming, dependnig on the accuracy of the typist
because typing errrors have be to corrected on
on each carbon copy. In many organisations carbon
copies are not longer used, and copies are now
made on the photo-copier.

20.5 Speed Development

Wor

Connecting a computer to its peripherals can be a   1
problem. Our combination set containing a wiring   2
kit, switching gear and twin earthing block makes   3
it all so easy. No special skills are necessary.   4

      1   2   3   4   5   6   7   8   9   10

Anyone can connect their electronic typewriter or   1
word processor to the power supply. All you have   2
to do is follow the diagrams and instructions and   3
your machines will be connected in just minutes.   4

      1   2   3   4   5   6   7   8   9   10

Chapter 21

The Use of Keys q and ,

Ascenders and Descenders

When we learnt to write, we made our first attempts on lined paper. We soon learnt that although the letters are written 'on the line' a number of letters have extensions that go below the line while others extend well above the line. The parts that extend above the line are known as *ascenders* (as with the letters **b, f, h**) whilst those which extend below the line are known as descenders (as with **q, p, g**).

Typewriter keys or print wheels print the letters with ascenders and descenders after the fashion of handwriting. However, some computer printers can only produce letters within the space allocated to a line, and the 'descenders' do not, in fact extend below the line but rest on it. This makes the text difficult to read.

There are also some computer systems that display text on the screen in this way, and this, too, is difficult to read. If you are buying a computer or a printer, this should be one of the factors you investigate before you buy.

21.1 Guidelines

The letter **q** key is the last key to be learnt on the top row of letter keys. It is situated at the top left of the row and is operated by the little finger of the left hand (the **a** finger). The **,** key (comma) is located on the bottom row of keys and is depressed with the middle finger of the right hand (the **k** finger).

Look at the keyboard to ensure that you learn to make the key reaches with confidence.

To depress the **q** key, place your fingers over the home keys and move the left hand upwards and to the left, keeping all your fingers slightly curved. Strike the **q** key with the little finger and *immediately* return all your fingers to the home keys.

To depress the **,** key, move your right hand downwards and to the left, keeping the fingers slightly curved. Strike the **,** key with the middle finger of the right hand and *immediately* return all your fingers to the home keys.

21.2 Exercises

Practise the key reach movements outlined in the guidelines without actually striking the keys. When you have gained the confidence to locate the new keys, practise the key reaches a few times without looking at the keyboard. Then practise the location drills and the word and sentence exercise. Type each line twice.

Location Drills

```
aq aq aq aq k, k, k, k, sq s, kq d, lq j, qu f, aq
aqa ;p; aqa lol sws kik ded aqa frf juj ftf jyj aq

k,k dcd l.l aqa fvf jmj fbf jnj fgf jhj aqa k,k k,
aq, aqu sq, squ qu, que aq, qua sq, quo dq, qui k,
```

Words

```
quit, aqua, quota, squad, quotes, queue, enquiries
qualify, acquire, question, squash, require, quick

unique, quantity, quite, square, equipment, quorum
quality, requests, quiet, acquaint, quest, queries
```

Sentences

```
It is really quite easy to operate this equipment.
You require a system disk and a good quality blank
user disk.  Input your unique password in response
to the screen query.  You will quickly become used
to the new equipment and gain your qualifications.
```

Although you may acquire the ability to type quite quickly on a manual typewriter, you will find that your keyboarding speed is quicker on an electronic machine. The keyboard is also very much quieter.

21.3 Tips

It is difficult to type with accuracy or at speed if your hands are cold, so always ensure that your hands are warm when you are using the keyboard. Some people who suffer from cold hands like to rub their fingers together thoroughly before starting to type in order to get the blood-flow circulating well.

Athletes always spend some time 'warming-up' before training or before a race, and pianists practise their scales before playing. In the same way, keyboard operators benefit from spending a few moments practising key location drills as a 'warm-up' before starting work.

21.4 Proof-reading

The following passage has been printed twice. The first copy has been typed correctly but the second copy contains typographical errors. Proof-read the second passage and see if you can identify all the errors. Your proof-reading skills may be checked against the key on p. 192.

Printer Transfer Switches
_____

Computer printers can be expensive, especially when acoustic hoods must also be bought to reduce noise. However, printer use is intermittent, most of the typist's time being taken with inputting data into the computer. Costs can be reduced if two typists share the same printer by use of a printer transfer switch.

Printer Transfer Switch
_____

Computer printers can be especailly when accoustic hoods must be be bought to reduce noise. However, printer use is intermittent most of the Typist's time being taken up with inputting data into the computer. Costs canbe reduced if two typists share the same printer by use of a printer printer transfere switch.

21.5 Speed Development

This new high quality spelling checker program is
unique because it is designed for use with almost
every make of computer equipment. Your secretary
will be able to check her work much more quickly.
Enquire today, or send a cheque with your orders.

1   2   3   4   5   6   7   8   9   10

Chapter 22

The Use of Keys z and x

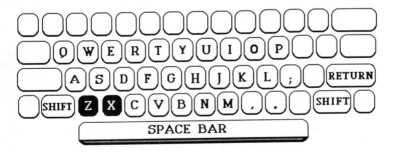

22.1 Guidelines

The letter **z** and **x** keys, which complete the bottom row of letter keys, are both situated to the left of the bottom row of keys. The letter **z** key is operated with the little finger of the left hand (the **a** finger) and the

105

letter **x** key is operated with the third finger of the left hand (the **s** finger). Look at the keyboard to ensure that you learn to make the key reaches with confidence.

To depress the **z** key, place your fingers over the home keys. Move the left hand downwards and to the right, keeping the fingers slightly curved. Strike the **z** key with the little finger of the left hand and *immediately* return all the fingers to the home keys.

To depress the **x** key, place your fingers over the home keys. Move the left hand downwards and to the right, keeping the fingers slightly curved. Strike the **x** key with the third finger of the left hand and *immediately* return all the fingers to the home keys.

22.2 Exercises

Look at the keyboard and practise the new key reaches as described in the guidelines until you can locate the keys with confidence. Start by practising the movements without actually striking the keys.

When you have gained confidence with the key reaches, practise the location drills, and the word and sentence exercises. Type each line or sentence twice.

Location Drills

```
az az az az sx sx sx sx lz kx za xs iz ux az sx jx
aza aza l.l l.l sxs sxs k,k k,k aqa aza sws sxs kx

aqaza ;p;p; swsxs lol.l dedcd kik,k frfvf jujmj jx
ftfbf jyjnj fgf jhj aza fsx sxs laz kax azk ize xo
```

Words

```
six mix box zoo axe zip exit size next text lazily
maze pixel dozen index prize zero axle haze gazing

matrix puzzles extra zones mixed zoom amazed taxed

experiences Teletext zapped Ceefax experts Teletex
excellent extremely complex mixture texture nozzle
```

Sentences

```
A screen graphics picture is made up of dozens of
tiny dots called pixels.  A high resolution screen
contains more pixels than a low resolution screen.
```

Some computer graphics programs are excellent and they are valued by artists for producing designs such as those used for television titles.

There are also extremely complex graphics programs used for computer aided design of equipment of all sizes such as aircraft and motor vehicles.

The videotex systems such as Teletex, Ceefax and Oracle also make use of graphics capabilities.

22.3 Tips

Keep your eyes on the text you are copying from as much as possible. If you use a manual typewriter practise the carriage return operation until you can carry it out quickly and sharply—and without moving your eyes from the text being copied. The movement should be made firmly and sharply, and you should return your left hand to the home keys immediately.

If you use an electric or electronic typewriter or a computer, practise pressing the return key without looking away from your copy, and always return your fingers to the home keys immediately. This simple movement is one of the factors in increasing speed, particularly as no time is wasted looking back to find the line you are copying from the draft.

22.4 Proof-reading

The following passage has been printed twice. The first copy has been typed correctly but the second copy contains typographical errors. Proof-read the second passage and see if you can identify all the errors. Your proof-reading skills may be checked against the key on p. 192.

Disk Care

Computer diskettes can pick up dust and dirt just like anything else in your office. Tiny particles of dirt on a diskette can result in scratches on the surface which results in loss of data. Magnetic fields found near your computer and telephone or other electrical equipment can corrupt data stored on a diskette. Always store diskettes in the special storage boxes available from office equipment companies.

Disk Care

Computer diskettes can pick up dust anddirt just li'
anything else in your office.   Tiny particals of di
on a diskette can result in scraches on the surface
which results in loss of dates.   Magnetic feilds
found near your computer or telephone or other
electrical equipment can corrupt data stored on a
on a disk.   Always store disks in the special
storeage boxes available from office equipment
companies.

22.5 Speed Development

Wc

If you use a computer or a word processor you will
appreciate the great flexibility offered by a word
processing program.   Documents are filed on a disk
and listed by name on the index.   Documents may be
recalled to the screen so that text can be edited.

1   2   3   4   5   6   7   8   9   10

Chapter 23
The Use of
Shift Lock, Caps Lock and :

Good Housekeeping

In computer terms, 'housekeeping' means the management, storage and control of disks and of the files and documents stored on the disks. Documents must be given logical names so that they can be identified with ease when required. A great deal of time can be wasted when you are searching for a particular document if you have to recall several documents to the screen before you identify the correct one.

Files and documents must also be copied from time to time, or deleted when they are no longer required. The term 'housekeeping' also refers to the duplication of 'back-up' disks in case the original disk is damaged or lost. It may also be necessary to set up passwords and controls on the disks as a security measure.

23.1 Guidelines

The : (the colon) is typed by holding down the shift key and striking the ; key (the semi-colon) with the little finger of the right hand. Move

109

the left hand down and slightly to the left so that you can hold down the *shift* key with your little finger, keeping all your fingers slightly curved. Strike the : key with the little finger of the right hand. Release the *shift* key and return the fingers of your left hand to the home keys.

To type a whole word or several words in capitals, activate the *shift lock* key, which is generally situated on the left side of the keyboard at the end of the home key row. Press down the *shift lock* key, which will stay 'locked' or activated. Return your fingers to the home keys and type the word(s) to be capitalised. To release the shift lock, press the *shift* key. Note that on some computer keyboards the shift lock is released, or de-activated, by pressing the *shift lock* key a second time.

If you are using a computer that does not have a *shift lock* key on the keyboard you should use the *caps lock key*, which is usually situated at the left of the keyboard close to the home row of keys. Remember that the *caps lock* key does not activate the symbols on the upper half of the number/symbol keys. If, for example, a colon occurs in the capitalised text (e.g., HOURS: TO BE ARRANGED), you must use the *shift key*. The *caps lock* key acts like a switch (called a *toggle switch* on a computer); it is pressed once to activate it, and a second time to release it.

On many computer and electronic typewriter keyboards, the *caps lock* and/or *shift lock* keys are provided with a small red light which indicates when they are 'on'.

23.2 Exercises

Look at the keyboard to practise the movements described in the guidelines until you feel confident enough to make the key reaches without looking. Then practise the location drills and the sentence exercises. Type each line or sentence twice.

Location Drills

;:; a:a ROM l:l s:s RAM d:d k:k CPU f:f j:j VDU ;:

frfvf jujmj dedcd kik,k swsxs lol.l aqaza ;p;:; a:

asdfgfa ;lkjhj; ftfgf jyjhj asdf ;lkj fbfgf jnjhj:

Sentences

```
How to pay: goods may be paid for in various ways.
By cheque: enclose the cheque with the order form.
By credit card: card number accepted by telephone.
On account: we will invoice you for goods ordered.
Settlement terms: six weeks after date of invoice.
```

```
The CPU of this machine contains a ROM chip: the
abbreviation ROM means READ ONLY MEMORY.
```

```
The CPU also contains a RAM chip: the abbreviation
RAM means RANDOM ACCESS MEMORY.
```

```
Information held in the ROM is retained even when
the computer is switched off: the RAM memory is
lost when the machine is switched off.
```

23.3 Tips

The *caps lock* key and the *shift lock* key perform different functions on a computer keyboard. The *shift lock* key is activated in order to type a whole word or several words in capitals. In addition, where a number and a symbol, or two symbols, are shown on one key, the upper symbol may be typed when the *shift lock* key is depressed. In order to type the figure keys on the top row, or the lower of two symbols, the *shift lock* key must be de-activated.

The *caps lock* key is also used to type a whole word or several words in capitals. However, the *caps lock* key changes only the lower case *alphabet* letters into upper case letters. It differs from the *shift lock* key because it does not affect the keys containing numbers, symbols and punctuation such as the colon. When the *caps lock* key has been depressed, the lower character shown on a number or symbol key will be printed. If you need one of the symbols shown on the upper half of the keys, you must press the *shift* key to obtain it. On some computer keyboards the *shift* key may be operated without de-activating the *caps lock* key.

23.4 Proof-reading

The following passage has been printed twice. The first copy has been typed correctly but the second copy contains typographical errors.

Proof-read the second passage and see if you can identify all the errors.
Your proof-reading skills may be checked against the key on p. 193.
    When you have finished proof-reading, type the first passage to gain
practice in typing longer paragraphs.

Paper Storage and Security

Paper storage is always a problem in an office.
As the amount and size of paper to be stored
increases, the amount and size of the storage
cabinets have to be increased, with the consequent
problem of where to site the storage cabinets.

Computers are said to offer the opportunity to
eliminate the paper storage problem by dispensing
with paper file copies and storing all file data
on disk, but this poses problems of security. It
is difficult for anyone to remove a whole filing
cabinet along with its files, but a disk, or even
a box of disks, is easily stolen or mislaid.

Storage and Security

Paper storeage is always a problem in an office.
As the amount and size of the storage cabinets
have to be increased, with the consequent problem
of where to sight the storage cabinets.

Computers are said to offer the the opportunity to
elimanate the paper storage problem, by dispensing
with paper copies and storing all file data on disk
but this poses the problem of security. It's
difficult for any one to remove a whole filing
cabinet along with its files, but a disk or even a
box of disks, is easily stolen or misled.

23.5 Speed Development

	Words
There are several ways in which messages are sent	10
by electronic mail facilities. Telex is a fairly	20
slow method, and messages are restricted to upper	30
case characters. Teletex is much quicker, and it	40
allows both upper and lower case characters. Fax	50
systems, short for facsimile, allow both text and	60
pictures to be transmitted but it is fairly slow.	70

1   2   3   4   5   6   7   8   9   10

Chapter 24

Figures Key Row

24.1 Guidelines

On the top row of keys the figures start at the left with **1** and progress to the right up to **9**, followed by the **0**. The easiest way to learn to type these figures is to move both hands up to the top row of keys to form a new 'temporary' home row. Move the hands up and slightly to the left,

114

keeping all the fingers slightly curved. Rest the fingers of the left hand over **1 2 3** and **4**, and the fingers of the right hand over **7 8 9** and **0**.

To type these figures the little finger of the left hand depresses **1**, the third finger **2**, the middle finger **3**, and the index finger **4** and **5**. The little finger of the right hand depresses **0**, the third finger **9**, the middle finger **8** and the index finger **7** and **6**.

To type the figure **5**, move the left hand slightly to the right, strike the figure **5** key with the index finger and *immediately* return the fingers to the **1 2 3** and **4** keys. To type the figure **6**, move the right hand slightly to the left, strike the figure **6** key with the index finger and *immediately* return the fingers to the **7 8 9** and **0** keys. Return the hands to the original **asdf jkl;** home row of keys as soon as you have finished typing the figure(s) required.

To type numbers containing a decimal point, type the first number(s), then move the hands back to the home row of keys. Type the full stop with the third finger of the right hand (the **1** finger). Return the fingers to the home row and then up to the figures row to complete typing the number.

In the early stages of keyboard learning, always move both hands to the figures row when typing the figures. In time you will find that you move only one hand to the figures key row for the appropriate figure keys whilst the other hand remains on the home keys. However, do not hurry to move to this stage until you have gained confidence and proficiency.

24.2 Exercises

Look at the keyboard and practise moving the hands up to the top figures row and back to the home keys, as described in the guidelines, without actually depressing any keys.

Practise moving the hands up to the top figures row, back to the home keys in order to type the full stop for the decimal point and then back to the top row of keys.

When you feel that you can locate the figure keys and move to the full stop for the decimal point with confidence, practise the location drills, figure practice and sentences. Type each line or sentence twice.

Location Drill

1234 0987 1 2 3 4 7 8 9 0 4321 7890 4321 7890 1470
454 767 454 767 4540 7671 123451 0987670 123456789

Figure Practice

```
18  19  10  17  16  01  06  03  20  05  29  38  37  40  46  54  67
517.88  11.25  493.75  6.333  265.38  270.05  73.18  3.52
```

Sentences

```
Deliver 80 computers and 40 printers to 95 Ardway.
Take 4 lots of 20 computers and 10 printers today.
Average sales were 270.5, 199.75, 328.5 and 410.5.

Fire safe 367 has 2, 3 or 4 drawers and 2 shelves.
Telephone 259 3469 and order 1,800 record holders.
Key in the data: 193.93, 297.44, 804.33 and 61.92.
```

24.3 Tips

If your typewriter does not contain the figure **0** (the zero), you should use the upper case **O**. If there is no figure **1** on the keyboard, use the lower case **l**.

When you use a computer, it is important to use the figure **1** and **0** keys for the numbers 1 and 0. If the letter **l** and capital **O** are used, the computer will not recognise them as figures when carrying out functions involving calculations, etc. The zero is generally shown on the screen with an oblique stroke through it, to differentiate it from the capital **O**.

When typing figures containing a decimal point, the full stop is used to represent the decimal point.

24.4 Proof-reading

The following passage has been printed twice. The first copy has been typed correctly but the second copy contains typographical errors. Proof-read the second passage and try to identify all the errors. Your proof-reading skills may be checked against the key on p. 193.

When you have finished proof-reading, type the first passage to gain practice in typing longer paragraphs.

Trimplex Micro Systems have launched the TXM 5755
microcomputer, a standalone computer based on an
Intel 8086 processor and incorporating 640 Kbytes
of host resident RAM. It also features 10 Mbytes
of Winchester disk storage, and a single 360 Kbyte
double sided, double density floppy disk drive.
The 14 inch colour monitor is adjustable for tilt,
swivel and slide. For further details telephone
552 397961 or write to Tony Skear, Department 927,
Trimplex Micro Systems, 72 South Vincent Street,
Glasgow, G4 3PQ.

Trimplex Micro Systems have launched the TXM 575
microcomputer, a stand alone microcomputer based on
an Intel 8086 processor and also incorporating
640 Kbytes of host resident Ram. It also features
10 Mbytes of winchester disk storeage, and a single
360 Kbyte double sided, double dynasty floppy disk
drive. The 4 inch colour monitor is adjustable fo_r
tilt, swivel and slides. For further details
telephone 552 397961 or write to Tony Skear,
Department 927, Trimplex MicroSystems, 72 South
Vincent Streeet, Glasgow, G4 3PQ.

24.5 Speed Development

Words

are interested in leasing a site on the Ryburn	10
ence Park. We need a total site space of over	20
hectares, with 30,000 square metres of factory	30
ce. We also require about 7,000 square metres	40
office space, with parking for lorries and for	50
s. Adequate room for expansion is essential.	60

    2   3   4   5   6   7   8   9   10

Chapter 25

The Numeric Key Pad

Introduction

The numeric key pad is an extra bank of keys located at the right of the keyboard on most computer keyboards. On some computers, the numeric key pad may also contain keys with mathematical symbols such as $+ - \div$ and $=$ as shown below.

The layout of the figure keys follows the standard calculator layout and generally includes a special key for the decimal point. The mathematical symbol keys usually surround the figure keys, but the actual position of each of these keys varies from machine to machine. In addition there is an *Enter* key that operates in the same way as the *Return* or *Enter* key on the main keyboard.

The numeric key pad is very useful for typists or operators who need to key in large amounts of numeric data.

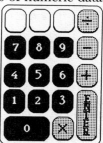

25.1 Guidelines

The secret of mastering the numeric key pad is to establish the figures **4**, **5** and **6** as a set of home keys. The index finger of the right hand should rest on the figure **4**, the middle finger on **5** and the third finger on **6**.

Use the index finger to reach up to the figure **7** and down to the figure **1**. The middle finger should be used to reach up to the figure **8** and down to the figure **2**. Use the third finger to reach up to the figure **9** and down to the figure **3**. The index finger may also be used to operate the figure **0** key.

The thumb of the left hand may be used to insert spaces between sets of numbers by pressing the space bar on the QWERTY keyboard.

It is not possible to give definite rules about which finger should be used for each of the mathematical symbol keys because their positions are not standardised. You will have realised by now that mastery of the keyboard depends on always using a particular finger to strike a given key. Analyse the positions of the mathematical symbol keys on your key pad and allocate an appropriate finger to strike each of these keys.

Practise the key reaches for these keys as you have done throughout this book until you can locate the keys confidently without looking at the key pad.

25.2 Exercises

Place the fingers of your right hand over the row of home keys on the numeric key pad as described in the guidelines, and ensure that you familiarise yourself with the key reaches for the figure keys.

Establish key reaches for the mathematical function keys as suggested in the guidelines. Look at the numeric key pad until you gain confidence, practising the key reaches several times without actually depressing the keys.

When you can locate the keys with confidence, practise the location drills. Leave a single letter space between sets of figures, and a single letter space each side of a mathematical symbol.

Location Drills

```
456 654 546 564 645 456 664 554 446 554 45654 6545
474 585 696 966 855 58564 47456 69654 749685 47586

414 525 636 144 255 366 47414 58525 69636 12345678
404 505 606 100 205 306 900 70.52 90.03 10.05 19.0

240 + 95 + 372 = 707.   170.525 + 290.034 = 460.559
357 - 410 = 53.   997 ÷ 13.5 = 73.85.   135 ÷ 15 = 9
47 x 17 = 799.   17.54 x 19.32 = 338.87.   7 - 3 = 4
```

25.3 Tips

If there is no numeric key pad on your keyboard, use the figures row on the QWERTY keyboard for the numbers. Use the lower case letter **x** with a space each side for the multiplication symbol, and the hyphen for the minus symbol.

25.4 Proof-reading

The following set of figures has been printed twice. The first copy has been typed correctly, but the second copy contains typographical errors. Proof-read the second passage and see if you can identify all the errors. Your proof-reading skills may be checked against the key on p. 193.

When you have finished proof-reading, type the first passage to gain practice in typing longer paragraphs.

471.55 582.96 693.70 339.84 102.73 950.32 493.11

392.39 568.10 302.01 112.83 884.72 239.06 676.66

321.49 550.03 600.02 774.00 908.67 330.15 667.67

471.55 588.96 696.70 339.84 102.73 953.32 493.11

393.39 568.10 302 01 112.83 884.7– 239.06 667.66

3210.49 50.03 600.02 112.83 908.67 330.15 667.66

25.5 Speed Development

Words

```
                                                              10
 Contec Exhibition offers a unique opportunity
examine and try out the latest developments in               20
puting.   At over 380 stands exhibitors will be              30
wing about 800 computers and related software.               40
```

```
   2      3      4      5      6      7      8      9     10
```

```
                                                              10
 exhibition will be held at the new Broadgrove
ibition Centre, London, on Monday, Tuesday and               20
esday, 16, 17,and 18 August.   It is open from              30
) hours to 1800 hours each day.   Send for your             40
  admission ticket today.   There is no charge.             50
```

```
   2      3      4      5      6      7      8      9     10
```

Chapter 26

Symbols and Fractions

 Symbols are those characters that are neither letters nor numbers. Computer keyboards and most electronic keyboards contain quite a wide variety of symbol characters, but the following examples are found on most keyboards:

*	Asterisk	"	Double quotation mark	/	Oblique stroke (slash)
@	At	'	Single quotation mark	–	Hyphen
£	Pound	(	Opening bracket	_	Underline
$	Dollar	)	Closing bracket	?	Question mark
¢	Cent	%	Per cent	#	Hash
+	Plus	=	Equals	!	Exclamation mark

In addition, there may be two or three keys containing fractions such as:

$$\tfrac{1}{4} \quad \tfrac{3}{4} \quad \tfrac{5}{8} \quad \tfrac{7}{8} \quad \tfrac{1}{3} \quad \tfrac{2}{3} \quad \tfrac{1}{2}$$

The position of these keys is not standard on typewriter or computer keyboards, and if you use two or three different keyboards regularly you may find that you always need to check the positions of these symbols by glancing at the keyboard before typing them.

26.1 Guidelines

The positions of the symbol and fraction keys are not standardised on the various keyboards available today, and it would be of limited value to give guidance on which finger should be used to strike a particular key.

You are by now aware that you use each finger for a specific set of keys, whose positions are logically related to the home key for each finger. Study the keyboard you are using to identify the position of each symbol. Where the symbols appear on the same key as a figure you will obviously use the same finger you use to strike that figure. It is likely that most of the remaining symbol keys will be positioned in such a way that the most logical finger to use is the little finger of the right hand.

Remember that where two symbols or fractions are displayed on each key, the uppermost symbol/fraction is typed by depressing the shift key while striking the key.

26.2 Exercises

Look at the keyboard until you gain confidence in making the key reaches. Identify the finger you will use for each character. Start with your fingers on the home keys and practise the movements required to locate each symbol without actually depressing the keys.

If the symbol is on the figure row of keys, move the appropriate hand up to the figure row (as previously described for typing the figures). Depress the *shift* key with the other hand, and strike the symbol key required. Release the *shift* key and return both hands immediately to the home row of keys.

Keep practising until you can locate each key without looking at the keyboard. If the symbol is on the same key as a number, make a conscious association between the two. This will help you to locate the key quite quickly. When you feel ready, type the exercises.

Have you seen our 'New-write' Pen? It features a slim-line barrel/shaft. Simply the best pen out!

Single 'New-write' pen @ £5.00 + VAT ($7 in USA).
Pack of pens @ £48.00 + VAT per box ($70 in USA).

We allow quantity discounts of 5% on 2 boxes, 10% on 5-10 boxes and 15% on for orders of 11+ boxes.

"New-write is the pen for me!" "It's just fine!"
Try one now! Write on this line _____

```
HERE ARE A FEW LINES FROM A COMPUTER PROGRAM
PRINT "START OF SUB-ROUTINE FOR NUMBERING FILES"
LET C = X * 100 INT (X3100)
IF G$ = B$(J) THEN PRINT "END OF FILE"
IF R - 2 * INT(R32) = O THEN GO TO 250
```

The # symbol is used in writing computer programs. In the USA the # symbol is used to represent the word "number", as in #4973, #2254, #3305 or #8849.

The pieces were 1¼" long by 2¾" wide by ⅝" deep. We require some pieces 16⅞" by 27⅓" by 5⅔" deep.

We made a profit of 22½% over the year, and we now propose to pay a dividend of 5½% to shareholders.

26.3 Tips

Some symbols have more than one use. The double and single quotation marks, for example, are used as symbols for inches and feet, e.g., 2′ 6″, and the following symbols are used within computer programs to indicate mathematical functions:

    *   Multiply   /   Division   +   Addition   −   Minus

The asterisk (*) is also used when giving a computer a command or instruction. These may be termed *star commands*, e.g., *CAT may mean display the catalogue (directory or index of documents) stored on the disk.

    If your computer keyboard does not possess fraction keys you may have to express the figures in decimal form, e.g., 5.5 for 5½ or 6.75 for 6¾. Alternatively, fractions may be shown by typing the two numbers which constitute the fraction and dividing them by an oblique stroke, e.g., 7/8. If a whole number precedes the fraction, such as 6⅓, leave a space between the whole number and the fraction, e.g., 6 1/3, when using the oblique stroke method.

    The exercises may be typed using either of these methods, but it will be necessary to use a longer line length because there will be more letter spaces to the line.

26.4 Proof-reading

The following passage has been printed twice. The first copy has been typed correctly but there are typographical errors in the second copy. Proof-read the second passage and see if you can identify all the errors. Your proof-reading skills may be checked against the key on p. 194.

When you have finished proof-reading, type the first passage to gain practice in typing longer paragraphs.

MoSta* Computer Desk

The MoSta* Computer Desk offers you the versatile workstation you have been waiting for! Here are just a few of its features: large enough to hold your computer and its peripherals; easy-moving MoGlide* castors; unique MoFeed* paper rack. Only £240 each + VAT ($360 in USA). The following quantity discounts apply (UK purchases only): 2 desks 5%, 5 desks 10%, 10 desks and above 15%.

* Registered Trade Name of Mosley-Steele PLC.

MoSta* Computer Desk

The MoSta Computer Desk offers you the vertasile workstation you have been waiting for. Here are just a few of its features: large enough to hold your computer and its perpherals; easy-moving MoGlide* castor; unique MoFeed* paper rake. Only - £250 each + Vat ($360 in USA). The following quality discounts apply (UK purchases only: 2 desks 5%, 5 desks 10%, 10 desks and over 15%.

* Registered Trade Mark of Mosley-Steele Ltd.

26.5 Speed Development

The use of fractions is disappearing and is being
replaced by the decimal system, but we still talk
about inches, feet, yards and miles. We now have
to buy our petrol in litres, but many of us still
think in terms of gallons. Even within the field
of computing disks are sized in inches and not in
centimetres, and there are 8", 5¼" and 3½" disks.

1   2   3   4   5   6   7   8   9   10

Chapter 27

Centring

You have learnt to use all the alphabet, number and symbol keys on the keyboard and are able to type any straightforward text. It is now time to learn the basic skills of layout or display, starting with centring headings and lines of text.

Headings or other items may be centred to draw attention to them or to provide an effective layout on the page. To give added emphasis you may leave one or two additional clear line spaces after headings or between a series of centred items.

You may provide some variation in the layout by typing the headings or other centred lines in a mixture of the following methods:

THIS IS TYPED IN CAPITALS

T H E S E   A R E   S P A C E D   C A P I T A L S

These are lower case letters

These Are Lower Case Letters With Initial Capitals

To type spaced capitals, leave one space between letters and three spaces between words.

27.1 Guidelines

Manual and electric typewriters
To centre a heading, move the typing point to the centre of the document (i.e. mid-way between the left and right margins). The table on p. 28 (Fig. 17) shows the number of character spaces across the

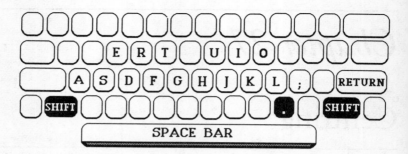

page for various type sizes. Divide this number by two to give the centre point of the paper. You may find it helpful to set a *tab* stop at this point. (Ensure that you clear any *tab* stops that may already be set before setting your *tab* stop. Refer to your manual for guidance on clearing and setting *tab* stops on your machine.)

It is important to use equal margins when centring headings or other items around the centre point of the page; refer to the table on p. 28 for guidance on margin sizes with the different sizes of type.

Press the tabulator key (Fig. 29) to move to the *tab* stop set at the centre point. Using the backspace key (Fig. 29), backspace *once* for every *two* letters or spaces in the heading or item you are centring. Ignore any odd letter left over. You are then at the starting point for typing the centred item.

FIG 29 Backspace key and tab key

Electronic typewriter

Most electronic typewriters have a special function key for automatic centring of headings or other items. As a rule the *centre* key is pressed and the text is typed, but it is not printed on the paper until the *return* key is pressed. The line of text is automatically centred by the machine. Check your machine manual for precise instructions.

Computer

Centring on computers falls into two categories. The system may not display the item on the screen in its centred position, and the centring operation is only carried out when the document is printed. A coded symbol is displayed on the screen on each side of the centred section of text to indicate that the command to centre has been given. These codes are termed 'embedded commands'. Although the codes show on the screen, they are not printed.

Alternatively, headings or other items may be displayed on the screen in their centred position, and this is obviously much more convenient for the typist, because the layout of the document can be seen on the screen as it will be printed out. Check your system user manual for instructions on using the centring function with your program.

27.2 Exercises

Follow the instructions in the guidelines before attempting these exercises. Centre each line. Type words in capitals or lower case as they are shown in the exercises. Type each exercise on a separate sheet of paper.

Exercise 1

COMPUTER SUPPLIES

Cleaning Kits
Copyholders
Dust Covers
Disks
Footrests
Labels
Modems

T O P   Q U A L I T Y

ORDER WITH CONFIDENCE

Exercise 2

FUNCTION KEYS

Insert
Delete
Help
Underline
Centre
Copy
Indent
Search and Replace
Cut and Paste
Embolden
Exit

Exercise 3

D A I S Y W H E E L   P R I N T   S T Y L E S

Bilingual Courier 10
Boldface Proportional Spaced
Courier 10
Courier 12
Elite Modern 12
Letter Gothic 12
Madeline Proportional Spaced
Majestic Cubic 10
Prestige Elite 12
Roman Proportional Spaced

27.3 Tips

Function keys differ from letter or figure keys in that they carry out
some task or function. The term is generally used in connection with
electronic typewriters and computers, but manual and electric
typewriters have keys that carry out functions, such as the shift key,
shift lock, backspace, margin setting keys, tab set and tab clear keys.
Most electronic typewriters have additional keys for functions such as
centring, underlining and emboldening.

The main function keys on a computer keyboard are:

1   The operational keys for carrying out functions such as return, enter, shift lock or caps lock.
2   A 'code' or 'command' or 'alt' (alternate) key, which activates a programmed function to allow an alphabet or number key to be used for an alternative purpose—to type a third character, or to carry out a function such as cursor movement.
3   Dedicated keys, programmed specifically to carry out functions such as search and replace, cut, paste, underline, centre, embolden or 'undo'. These keys are frequently found on dedicated word processors.
4   Programmable keys, or 'user definable' keys, which form a fifth row at the top of the QWERTY keyboard on some computers (Fig. 26, p. 47). They may be programmed by the user to carry out specific functions. Instructions for using these keys will be found in your user manual.

27.4 Proof-reading

The following passage has been printed twice. The first copy has been typed correctly but there are typographical errors in the second copy. Proof-read the second passage and see if you can identify all the errors. Your proof-reading skills may be checked against the key on p. 194.

When you have finished proof-reading, type the first passage to gain additional practice in centring items.

W A V E N E Y   S Y S T E M S

OUR COMPANY SERVICES INCLUDE

Leasing Contracts
Lease Rental and Hire Purchase
Customised Database Systems
Maintenance and Service Contracts
Installation Contracts
Network Systems and Multi-User Systems

DEMONSTRATION AND SECOND-USER MACHINES AVAILABLE

W A V E R L Y   S Y S T E M S

YOUR COMPANY SERVICE INCLUDES

Lease Contracts
Lease Rental and Hire-Purchase
Customer Data Base Systems
Maintainance and Service Contracts
Instalation contracts
Net-work Systems and Multi User Systems

DEMONSTRATION AND SECOND-HAND MACHINES AVAILAIBLE

27.5 Speed Development

Wor

If you find it difficult to read the text display	1
on the screen of your computer, it may be because	2
the brightness control has been set too low. The	3
majority of computers have some means of allowing	4
the user to adjust the brightness of the display,	5
and some also have a contrast control. Remember,	6
faulty adjustment may lead to eyestrain problems.	7

1   2   3   4   5   6   7   8   9   10

Chapter 28

Underlining and Emboldening

Headings and other items may be emphasised by underlining, which is sometimes referred to as underscoring. On a typewriter underlining is achieved by use of the underscore symbol, which is usually positioned on the same key as the figure 6. Underlining is carried out on a computer by means of a special word processing function. Underlining should start directly beneath the first letter of the heading and finish directly beneath the final letter.

If you use a computer, emphasis may also be added by the use of bold print, or emboldening. The emboldened letters are struck twice when the printing process takes place, the second time being slightly to the right of the first time the letter is printed so that the words appear blacker than the rest of the text.

Headings and words within the text may be both underlined and emboldened, if desired, as shown in the example below.

<u>COMPUTER MEMORY</u>

Computers have two types of internal memory:

<u>ROM</u> and <u>RAM</u>. <u>ROM</u> stands for **Read Only Memory.**

<u>RAM</u> is an acronym for **Random Access Memory.**

28.1 Guidelines

Manual, electric and electronic typewriters

Type the heading or other item to be underlined. *Without* pressing the return key, use the backspace key to backspace to the start of the word(s) to be underlined. Press down the shift lock key and strike the underscore key the appropriate number of times to bring the underscore to the end of the text being underlined. An electric or electronic typewriter is usually fitted with a repeat key mechanism which allows you to hold down the underscore key until the underline is of the desired length.

Emboldening is not possible on a manual or electric typewriter, but some electronic typewriters have this facility. If you use an electronic typewriter, check your user manual for instructions.

Computer

Underlining of text on a computer is done through the underline function. As described for the centring function, the underline is either displayed on the screen as it will be printed, or it is not shown on the screen, embedded printing codes being used to indicate that the text will be underlined when it is printed. On some systems the heading is typed first, the cursor returned to the start of the heading and the instruction to underline given. Other systems allow the headings to be underlined at the same time as they are typed.

The procedure for emboldening text is similar to that for underlining. Where text is displayed on the screen exactly as it will be printed out, the emboldened text will be highlighted on the screen so that it is easily identified as bold print. Where embedded printer commands are used the emboldening will be carried out when the printing takes place.

Text may be centred, underscored and emboldened, if desired. Check your user manual for instructions on using these functions on your system.

28.2 Exercises

Follow the instructions given in the guidelines together with the appropriate details in your machine instructions manual before attempting this section. Type the exercises below, underlining headings and other items as shown. Add bold print as shown, if the emboldening function is available on your machine. Type each exercise on a separate sheet of paper.

Exercise 1

NEW COMPUTING DICTIONARIES

Two new dictionaries, dealing with the area of New Technology, have recently come onto the market. They are both available through Dictology Press.

Learn the Right Term - Computing Dictionary

This comprehensive book by Chris Rydolski contains 1,500 clearly-explained computing terms. It is ideal for the beginner in computing.

Think Right in Business Computing

The executive trying to cope with business affairs and at the same time plough through computing "jargon" will find this dictionary by Jean Friar invaluable. It contains 3,200 business computing terms, explained in straightforward language.

Exercise 2

ELECTRONIC MAILING AND MODEMS

To send a message by electronic mail your computer must be linked to a **MODEM** (the term is formed from the words **MO**dulator/**DEM**odulator). Your telephone hand-set is also linked to the **MODEM** in order to transmit the message. Incoming messages are received by the same process, through a **MODEM**.

Exercise 3
COMPUTER SOFTWARE FOR EDUCATION AND TRAINING

Compushop   A business game that simulates the many problems facing the manager of a retail shop. It is suitable for most disk operating systems, and is offered at the new <u>low price</u> of £30 + **VAT**.

Compuwork   A program to help school-leavers trace their way through a maze of real-life choices in the search for a job. Compuwork is suitable for most disk operating systems, and is offered at the new <u>extra low price</u> of £19.99 + **VAT**.

28.3 Tips

If you want to achieve a professional result it is important to display your text consistently throughout a document. On a long document margins should be set at the same point on successive pages, and the page number should be typed in the same position on each page. You should consistently leave a clear line space between paragraphs so that your document is easy to read.

Many typewriting textbooks are available to help you develop your typing skills after the keyboard has been mastered, but you can learn a great deal through simple observation. Whenever you read newspapers, magazines, reports and business letters, examine the way in which the information is laid out on the page, and the way in which 'white space' is used. This will help you to develop a 'sense of display'.

28.4 Proof-reading

There are a number of errors in the following passage. Proof-read the passage and see if you can identify all the errors. Your proof-reading skills may be checked against the key on p. 195.

Type a correct copy of the passage for additional practice in centring, underlining and emboldening.

COMPUTERS IN HOTELS

The large hotel groups have been useing computers for some years. Owner's of many of the country's smaller hottels have now realised that a computer can improve efficiency in there establishment. Interest has now increased to sucha level that computer exhibitions are devoted to the neeeds of the hotel industry. Softwear is available for all aspects of the trade including the following:

Advance Reservations

Depposits
Booking Charts
Correspondnence

Arrivals and Departures

Geust Accounts
Daily Balancing
Customised Analysis

Guest History

Selective Search
mailshots
Repeat Bookingings

28.5 Speed Development

Words

rd processing involves all the skills of typing	10
us the application of many display features and	20
nctions, some of which are quite complicated. A	30
ally proficient word processor operator is very	40
ghly skilled, particularly if he or she is able	50
apply his/her skills to a variety of machines.	60

1   2   3   4   5   6   7   8   9   10

Chapter 29

Paragraph Layout

 The three types of paragraph layout used in typewriting are *blocked,* *indented,* and *hanging paragraphs.* Examples of each of these styles are shown below:

```
BLOCKED STYLE  This is the most commonly-used form
of paragraph layout.  All the lines in the paragra
start at the left hand margin.  Blocked styled
paragraphs are quick and easy to use.


     INDENTED STYLE  The first line of text starts
five letter spaces in from the left hand margin.
All other lines in the paragraph start at the left
hand margin.


HANGING STYLE  The first line of a hanging paragra
  starts at the left hand margin, whilst all other
  lines are indented two letter spaces from the le
  margin.
```

Leave one clear line space between paragraphs (i.e. press the return key twice).

29.1 Guidelines

Blocked style paragraphs

Blocked style paragraphs are the easiest and quickest to type, and you are recommended to use this style for the majority of your work.

Always start by clearing away any tab stops that have been set. Check your user manual for details on setting and clearing tab stops.

138

Indented paragraphs

To type indented paragraphs, set a tabulator stop five spaces in from the left margin. At the start of each paragraph press the tab key to move to the tab stop position you have set and type the paragraph. Remember that all following lines start at the left margin. Refer to your user manual for instructions on setting tabs.

Hanging paragraphs

The method of typing hanging paragraphs differs on typewriters and computers.

If you use a typewriter, set a tabulator stop two spaces in from the left margin. Start to type the first line of the text at the left margin. After pressing the return key/lever at the end of the first line of text, press the tab key to move to the tab stop position you have set. Do this for each following line in the paragraph.

If you use a computer, use the indent function to inset the second and following lines of text when using hanging paragraph style. Refer to your system manual for instructions.

29.2 Exercises

Read the guidelines before attempting these exercises. Use blocked, indented or hanging paragraph style as shown. Type each exercise on a separate sheet of paper.

Exercise 1

You may have heard of 'Desk Top Publishing' in connection with new technology. The term refers to the manipulation of text, pictures and graphics on the VDU screen.

A special software program is required and a laser printer is generally used to produce printed material of a high quality.

Desk Top Publishing can be used to produce a page of a book, newpaper, advertising material, company newsletter, etc. The material may be intended for internal publication within the company, or for more general publication.

Exercise 2

Voice messaging is a developing area of new technology. Even if the person you are calling is not available a telephone messages can be left on the system.

The recipient can access the message at any time of the day or night from any telephone by use of a special unit.

If desired a single telephone message can be distributed to a number of recipients, instead of telephoning each one individually.

Exercise 3

As large organisations are faced more and more with
    the need to cut overheads, both in plant costs
    and wages, they are looking for alternatives to
    conventional employment.

Some companies are encouraging their staff to work
    from home using various elements of the new
    technology.

This approach is particularly successful in jobs
    where the member of staff does not need to be in
    the office to carry out his or her work.

Other companies help their employees to set-up in
    business on their own account. Sometimes they
    provide equipment and advice on running a
    business. They then contract work out to their
    ex-employee.

29.3 Tips

Many large companies decide upon a particular paragraph style for all letters, memoranda, reports, etc., typed within the organisation. Standardised layouts of this type are known as 'house style'. Organisations following this practice have a 'house style manual' which lists the layout styles to be followed by all typists. Make sure you enquire whether there is a 'house style manual' whenever you start a new job, whether you are a typist or a member of the management staff responsible for preparing correspondence or reports.

29.4 Proof-reading

The following passage has been printed twice. The first copy has beeen typed correctly but there are typographical errors in the second copy. Proof-read the second passage and see if you can identify all the errors. Check your proof-reading skills against the key on p. 196.

Type a correct copy of the passage for additional practice in typing indented paragraphs.

PARAGRAPHING

    Some people believe that paragraphs should be no longer than 15 lines, but it is difficult to be too precise. Certainly, very long paragraphs are likely to deter the reader. Short paragraphs of two or three lines long give emphasis, but the value of this is lost if too many short paragraphs are used.

    Never have the first line of a paragraph at the end of a page. If this is likely to happen, start the paragraph on a continuation sheet. It is easier to read and understand if there are at least three lines of text at the end of a page with the rest of the paragraph continued on a separate sheet.

PARAGAPHING

Some people beleive that paragraphs should be no longer that 5 lines, but it is difficult to be to be to precise. Certainly, very long paragraphs are likley to deter the reader. Shortparagraphs of two or three lines long give emphas is, but the valve of this is lost if too many short paragraphs are used.

Never have the first line of a paragraph at the end of the page. If this is likely to happen, start the paragraph on a continuation sheet. It is is easier to read and understand if there are at least 3 lines of text at the end of a end of a page with the rest of the paragraph continued on a seperate sheet.

29.5 Speed Development

Wo

The company provides a very wide range of welfare benefits for employees. The staff social club is open every evening of the week, and for the whole day on Saturdays and Sundays. Many social events and sporting activities are organised every year.

1   2   3   4   5   6   7   8   9   10

Temporary staff are invited to these functions so that they can get to know everyone and feel 'part of the family'. This year we plan a spring visit to the Dutch bulb fields, a summer day-cruise and disco, a barn dance and a Christmas dinner-dance.

1   2   3   4   5   6   7   8   9   10

Chapter 30

Justified Right Margin of Text

A very professional-looking document can be produced when using a word processing program on a computer by printing the text with a justified right margin. Word processing programs allow text to be printed out with a choice of a *ragged* right margin or a *justified* right margin. When a ragged right margin is used the text is printed like the layout produced on a manual typewriter, as shown in the example below:

```
This text has been printed with a ragged right
margin.  Some of the lines are longer than
others.  This produces what some people consider
is a slightly 'untidy' effect at the right
margin.
```

A justified right margin produces text with a completely even right margin which gives a neat and symmetrical appearance to the text. The system inserts additional spaces between words to ensure that the end of each line finishes at the same scale point to produce an even right margin.

```
This  is  an  example  of  text  printed  with  a
justified right margin.  If you receive a letter
with a justified right margin you may be fairly
sure  that  the  writer  owns  a  computer  or
dedicated word processor.
```

On most computers it is possible, within one document, for sections of text to be printed with both ragged and justified right margins.

30.1 Guidelines

Typewriters

It is not possible to achieve an automatically-justified right margin to text when using a manual or electric typewriter. Some electronic typewriters equipped with external memory capabilities may be able to produce a justified right margin to the text. If your electronic typewriter has this facility, refer to your system manual for instructions on using the function.

Computer

On some computers the word processing program produces a right justified margin as the default setting. If, for any reason, a ragged right margin is desired a command must be given to the computer to change from the justified default setting to a ragged right margin.

Other computers have a ragged right margin as the default setting and an instruction must be given to change to a justified right margin setting. This may be done by inserting a symbol on the ruler line (such as J for justified or R for ragged). Alternatively the text may be typed with a ragged right margin and the text to be justified may be highlighted to indicate to the system that this section of text is to be justified. If your system does not have a justified right margin as the default setting, you are recommended to read your user manual to ascertain the correct procedures.

30.2 Exercises

Read the guidelines before attempting these exercises.

Exercise 1

Type the paragraphs with a justified right margin.

A FLEXIBLE APPROACH TO TYPING

In the earlier part of this century typists learnt to use a manual typewriter and nothing else, because until electric typewriters came on the scene only manual typewriters were available.

Although there were many different forms of manual typewriter, their keyboards and the method of using them were very similar. Once a person had learnt

to type she (or he) could feel quite confident,   on
entering a new office,   that there would be no
problem about using the typewriter that was there.

Today's office may contain manual,   electric and
electronic typewriters,   along with a number of
different types of computer.   The typist therefore
needs to have a flexible approach to the use of
office keyboard equipment.

Exercise 2

Type the following passage, using ragged and justified right margins
for alternate paragraphs as shown (if this is possible on your
equipment).

Facsimile (often abbreviated to FAX) is a method of
electronic communication whereby a copy of a
document can be sent to a remote location (the
other side of the city or even the other side of
the world) at high speed over standard telephone
lines.

Documents containing typewritten text,   detailed
figures,   drawings,   plans,   printed matter and
handwriting (including signatures) can be sent to
the remote location in less than one minute.
Because the information does not have to be keyed
in,   FAX can claim to be one of the fastest methods
of accurate communication by electronic means.

Facsimile is useful because the original document
is simply fed into the machine where it is scanned.
Very little training is necessary because the
equipment is so simple to use, and skilled
personnel are not required to operate it.

30.3 Tips

The right margin is justified by the addition of extra spaces between words on most computers. This means that in many instances the system will insert extra spaces after punctuation such as the comma and the full stop. Although you may leave the recommended one space after a comma and two spaces after a full stop, you may therefore find that the program has adjusted this spacing in order to justify the right margin.

Note that where the last line of a paragraph is a 'part line', *followed by a return,* the system does not attempt to justify the line. Ensure that you always press the return key at the end of a paragraph, including the last paragraph.

30.4 Proof-reading

The following passage has been printed twice. The first copy has been typed correctly but there are typographical errors in the second copy. Proof-read the second passage and see if you can identify all the errors. Your proof-reading skills may be checked against the key on p. 196.

When you have finished proof-reading, type the first passage to gain additional practice. Centre the heading and the 'Catalogue Number' items as shown. Justify the right margin if this is possible on your equipment

```
              'FLEXXETTE' DISK FILING CABINETS

Did you know that it is now possible to buy special
filing cabinets especially for your floppy disks?
We provide a range for all sizes of disks:

        Catalogue Number FDF/210 for 8" disks
        Catalogue Number FDF/40 for 5¼" disks
        Catalogue Number FDF/95 for 3½" disks

Each cabinet holds up to 100 disks and has 10
dividers.   As a special promotional incentive we
are offering a 5% reduction on single orders and
12½% on orders of 5 or more cabinets (while present
stocks last only).  Send for a price list today!
```

'FLEXETTE' DISK FILEING CABINETS

Do you know that it is now possible to buy special fileing cabinets especially for your floppy disks. We provide a range forall sizes of disks;

Catalogue Number FDF/21 for 8' disks
Catalogue Number FDF/40 for 5¾" disks
Catalogue Number FDF/95 for 3½" disks

Each cabinet holds up to 100 disks and has 100 dividers. As a special promotional incentive we are offerring a 5 % reduction on single orders and and 12½% on orders of 5 or more cabinets (whilst present stocks last only). Send for a price list today?

30.5 Speed Development

Words

	Words
₂ most common complaint about computers is that	10
₂ instruction manuals provided for the hardware	20
₁ the software are difficult to understand. If	30
₁uals were written clearly and set out in a way	40
₂ reader could understand, the companies set up	50
provide training would have no customers. The	60
:uation is quite the opposite, however, and the	70
₁ber of training courses being offered by firms	80
₂cialising in this field are increasing weekly.	90

₁ 2 3 4 5 6 7 8 9 10

Chapter 31

Division of Words at the End of a Line

So far you have been given instructions about the margins or the line length to be used when typing exercises. From now on you should decide for yourself what size of margins should be used (unless you are given specific instructions for a particular exercise). This means that if you are using a typewriter you now have to make your own decisions about where to end each line of type. If you use a computer, these decisions will be made for you because the system will use the wraparound or wordwrap function.

A rather untidy appearance can be produced when using a ragged right margin if long words are allowed to extend beyond the set margin position, or if they are taken down to the next line, as shown in the example below.

```
The typist is involved with text display (or layout
The display of text has improved since
interchangeable typeheads were introduced.  They ar
particularly useful when typing technical or
scientific documents containing scientific symbols.
```

Even if you use a computer with a wraparound function and a justified right margin, the insertion of too many extra blank spaces across the line in order to justify a short line of text may produce an 'overspaced' effect, as shown below.

```
The typist is involved with text display (or layout
The    display    of    text    has    improved    sin
interchangeable typeheads were introduced.   They a
particularly   useful   when   typing   technical
scientific documents containing scientific symbols.
```

A better appearance may be obtained by dividing a long word between two lines. Two examples are shown below with words divided at the end of lines.

```
The typist is involved with text display (or layout).
The display of text has improved since interchange-
able typeheads were introduced.  They are particu-
larly useful when typing technical or scientific
documents containing scientific symbols.
```

```
The typist is involved with text display (or layout).
The display of text has improved since interchangeable
able typeheads were introduced.    They are particu-
larly  useful  when  typing  technical  or  scientific
documents containing scientific symbols.
```

Note that a hyphen is typed immediately after the first part of the word to indicate that it is continued on the next line.

31.1 Guidelines

Manual/electric/electronic typewriters
A warning bell (or 'beep') sounds to indicate that the typing point is about ten letter spaces from the right margin stop position. The actual number of spaces varies on different machines, and you should count the number of spaces available after the bell sounds on your typewriter. When the bell rings you can make a decision as to whether the word(s) to be typed next will fit on the line before the margin stop comes into action.

If the word to be typed is too long to fit on the line you may press the *margin release* key, which allows typing to continue into the right margin space. Alternatively, you may divide the word, typing a hyphen after the first part of the word, and take the remaining part down onto the next line..

Some electronic tyepwriters may have an *automatic return* function that returns the carriage and advances the paper by a line space when the typing point is within the bell zone.

Computer

Computers allow the use of hard and soft hyphens. The *hard hyphen,* which is usually inserted by striking the hyphen key on the keyboard, remains in the word no matter where the word is positioned on the line. It is used only when a word is to be permanently hyphenated, e.g., day-to-day or key-codes. The *soft hyphen* is used when dividing a word at the end of a line. If, at a later stage, additional words are inserted in the text so that the divided word no longer appears at the end of the line, the program automatically removes the hyphen.

If you were to use a hard hyphen to divide a word at the end of a line and at a later stage added extra wording which moved the divided word to the middle of a line, the hard hyphen would still appear in the middle of the word. Check with your user manual for instructions on the use of the hyphenation function on your system; this will give details on how to insert both hard and soft hyphens.

31.2 Exercises

Read the guidelines before attempting these exercises.

Exercise 1

Type this exercise as shown to give you practice in dividing words at the end of a line.

```
Computing is a dynamic industry.  Our represen-
tatives regularly attend training courses to ensure
that their knowledge is continually up-dated as the
specifications of existing products are improved
and new ones are introduced.  It is almost imposs-
ible to predict the direction in which computer
software manufacturers will move.  In addition,
computer software, technology and communications
are almost daily becoming increasingly sophisti-
cated, as can be seen from the new generation of
personal computers.
```

Exercise 2

Make your own decisions about margin sizes and line endings. *If necessary,* divide words at the end of lines to achieve an effective layout. If you use a word processing program, use hard or soft hyphens as appropriate.

Many people involved in management, design work, manufacturing or engineering find that communication is one of the most important abilities demanded in their jobs. In all kinds of business, and in the new technology fields in particular, effective oral and written communication is an essential skill. The importance of adequate training in communication skills cannot be over-stressed.

Many situations that may appear to be technical problems are often a matter of ineffective or defective communication rather than inadequate or badly-designed technology. Communication, whether oral or written, should be clear and accurate, and should use vocabulary suited to the level of the listener or reader. The correct technical terms must be used, of course, but wherever possible the use of 'jargon' should be avoided.

31.3 Tips

Divide a word at the end of a line so that the meaning of the word is clear, e.g., divide 'understand' as 'under-stand' and not as 'unde-rstand'. In general, make the division according to the sound and the sense of the word when it is spoken aloud. It is sensible to avoid dividing large numbers, such as 175,543,760, sets of figures such as 12,987-14,665 or 7 cm x 4 cm x 2 cm, or names such as Mr A J P Kingslaughton.

As a rule it is better to have a slightly ragged right margin than to divide too many words at line ends, partly because divided words tend to get in the way of easy communication and partly because it is not worth spending too much time thinking about whether or not to divide a word.

31.4 Proof-reading

The following passage contains some typographical errors. Proof-read the passage and see if you can identify all the errors. Your proof-reading skills may be checked against the key on p. 197.

When you have finished proof-reading, type a correct copy. Decide on your own margin sizes and line endings. Use double line spacing for the first and last paragraph and single line spacing for the second paragraph, as shown.

<u>W H I T E   S P A C E</u>

The area of a page of text on which their is no

typing is known as 'white space'. The creationof

white space around a paragraph or section of text

-helps to emphasise that paragraph or section so

that it stands out from the rest of the text.

White space can be created by increasing the mar -

gin sizes all round, and the line spacing between

items or paragraphs,

> Sections of text may aslo be indented (or
> inset(five or more spaces from both the
> left and right margins to pro vide added
> emphasis and to give an effective layout.

T
 he effect of white space may also be achieved by

varying the line spacing of the text. The main

portion of the text, for example, may be typed in

double line spacing, with sub-paragraphs typed in

Single line spacing, as in this passage.

31.5 Speed Development

Words

use of white space when displaying text helps   10
avoid an overcrowded appearance, and therefore   20
oves the appearance of the layout.   The white   30
e also provides emphasis and helps to attract   40
reader's attention to sections or paragraphs.   50

   2   3   4   5   6   7   8   9   10

ertain documents white space is left in order   10
ive the reader the opportunity to write notes   20
omments.   A draft report, for example, may be   30
d in treble line spacing, with two clear line   40
es between lines of type, so that alterations   50
mendments can be written clearly in the space   60
lable.   An agenda for a meeting may have very   70
margins and extra line spaces between agenda   80
s so that notes can be made of any decisions.   90

   2   3   4   5   6   7   8   9   10

Chapter 32

Letters

If you wish to type a formal letter to a company or other organisation, you should follow the conventional style of layout used in business letters, as described in this chapter.

32.1 Parts of the Letter

1 Reference details

When replying to a letter from a business organisation you may find that reference details have been included at the top of the letter. This usually gives the initials of the person writing the letter followed by those of the typist. It may also include file reference or account details, e.g., GKW/4779–K/JDS. You are expected to include this reference on your reply against the words 'Your ref' or 'Your reference'. If you wish to add reference details of your own, type these against the words 'Our ref' or 'My ref'.

2 Date

Always include the date on which the letter is typed. Type the date in the following form: 12 January 1988 or 5 May 1992.

3 Names and addresses

It is essential to include the name and address of the person sending the letter. The letter needs to be authenticated by the signature of the sender, and it is helpful to the recipient if you type your name in full at the end of the letter, particularly if your signature is difficult to decipher.

You should always keep a copy of any business correspondence in case you need to refer to it again at a later date, and it is therefore important to include the name and address of the person to whom you are writing (the addressee).

4   Courtesy opening and close

The traditional opening (or salutation) to a letter is 'Dear Sir' (or 'Dear Madam'), or 'Dear Mr ____' (or 'Dear Mrs/Miss/Ms ____') with the surname of the addressee included, If you know the addressee personally you may wish to start the letter informally with the person's first name, e.g., 'Dear Paul'. The letter will end with a *complimentary close*, usually 'Yours faithfully'. If you know the person, and particularly where the salutation includes the person's first name, you may use 'Yours sincerely'. Note that 'faithfully' and 'sincerely' start with lower case letters.

5   Body of the letter

The main part of the letter may start with a 'subject heading' to identify the topic of the letter. Use fairly short paragraphs in single line spacing, with a clear line space between paragraphs.

6   Enclosures

When other documents are sent with a letter, a reference to this is made by typing 'Enc' (abbreviation for enclosure) at the bottom of the letter.

7   Continuation sheets

When a letter covers more than one page, the additional pages are referred to as continuation sheets. You may wish to indicate the presence of a continuation sheet by typing 'Continued…' or 'PTO' at the bottom of the first page, but this is not really necessary because it is clear that the letter continues if there is no complimentary close and signature. The continuation page should contain the page number, the date and the name of the addressee.

8   File copy

As mentioned above, it is important to keep a record of business correspondence by taking a file copy. The procedure for taking copies is discussed in Chapter 33.

32.2 Guidelines

Layout of business letters

Stationery

You may have letter-headed paper printed with your address and telephone number. However, personal headed stationery is often printed on fairly small sheets of paper. You may therefore prefer to use the standard business size of A4 paper for your correspondence, with your address and (if appropriate) telephone number typed at the top of the page.

Line spacing

Type the addressee's name and address in single line spacing. Leave at least one clear line space between the various items on the letter. If the letter is short you may like to leave two clear line spaces between items as far as the salutation (i.e. turn up three times), as shown on the sample letter on p. 157.

Leave four clear line spaces (or more, depending on the size of your writing) between the complimentary close and your name in which to write your signature.

Punctuation

Modern business practice tends towards the use of what is known as the *open punctuation* style. This means that all non-essential punctuation, e.g. in names, addresses and abbreviations, is omitted, as shown on the sample letter on p. 157. However, if a place name or a person's name contains a hyphen or an apostrophe that is part of the name, this should be included, even when you use open punctuation style. Punctuation such as commas and full stops are, however, required in continuous text.

Paragraph layout

Use blocked style paragraphs with one clear line space between paragraphs.

Sample letter layout

Type a copy of this sample letter, following the layout and line spacing shown.

45 Grange Lane
Woodover St Mary's
Norfolk
PE35 7QB

My ref JB/5525-Mod

22 March 19--

The Sales Manager
Department PCEC/11
Compute-Right Systems Ltd
194-198 Cable Street
Birmingham .
B26 4TB

Dear Sir

Please send me a copy of your booklet 'Making the Most of Modems', as advertised in this month's 'Personal Computers and Electronic Communications' magazine. As requested, I enclose a cheque for £1.50.

Will you please also send me information about your range of modems, together with a price list.

I have a Cambrange 5525 personal computer. I should like specific details about modems to suit this equipment, and would appreciate any advice you can give me about fitting a modem to this type of computer.

Yours faithfully

Jeremy Baxter

Enc

32.3 Exercises

Read the guidelines before attempting these exercises. Use plain A4 paper and decide on your own margin sizes and line endings. Type the address at the top of the page as shown, and include today's date.

                              1 The Maze
                            Welfare Avenue
                               OXFORD
                              OX6 3EL

Today's date

Mr Gerrard O'Kelly
Busimans Service Company Ltd
International House
Jasmine Avenue
Maidenhead
Berkshire
SL6 9BR

Dear Mr O'Kelly

Thank you for your estimate for alterations to the central heating
system at the above address. I confirm that I am fully in
agreement with the price of £540 for the work as set out in your
estimate.

As discussed on the telephone today, I should like you to start
the work next Monday, 9 February, as I shall be leaving for a
six-week trip to Canada at the end of the month and want to be
sure the work is completed before I leave.

Yours faithfully

R G J AL-ANZI

32.4 Tips

If you use printed letter-headed stationery, hold the paper with the printed heading downwards and facing away from you. When you roll it through the roller the printed heading will be facing you. Turn up two or three times after the last line of the heading before starting to type. If you use a computer, remember to alter the top margin space to allow for the depth of the printed heading on the page – check your user manual for instructions.

The memory capacity of computers and some electronic typewriters enables you to create a document containing the standard parts of your letter. You can set up the margins and line spacing format and type in your address. When you are ready to type a letter, make a copy of this document and recall it to the screen. This has time-saving advantages.

32.5 Proof-reading

The following letter contains some typographical errors. Proof-read the letter and see if you can identify all the errors. Your proof-reading skills may be checked against the key on p. 198.

When you have finished proof-reading, type the letter correctly to gain additional practice.

29TH June

Miss Julie A Martin
67 White Acre
Saughall Bridge
Birmingham
B32 3PY

Dear Miss Martin

'PERM—A—TYPE' TYPEWRITER RIBBONS

Thank you for your intrest in our new range of typewriter ribbons
We produce three types of ribbon, each of which is suitable for you
'Bravenue' electronic typwriter.

The 'Everlasting' fabric ribbon, code PT/EL3, costs only £2.95, an
is suitable for the majority ofwork you are likely to produce
However, when you wish to impress your correspondent you should us
use one of our plastic carbon film ribbons.   The single—strik
crabon ribbon, code PT/SS3, gives a sharp image and costs only £387
The multi— strike carbon ribbon, code PT/MS3, costs a little more a
$4.66, but it lasts much longer.

Prices quoted are per ribbon.   The mimimum order size is fiv
ribbons of any one type.   We enclose an order form for yuou
convenience.Please be sure to quote the code number wen ordering.

Yours Sincerley
CAPITAL PERIPHERAL SUPPLIES LTD

Marjory Scruby (Mrs)
Supplies Manager

Enc

32.6 Speed Development

Words

: range of vinyl floor tiles has been specially   10
;igned for commercial areas. They are pleasant   20
look at, easy to maintain and yet surprisingly   30
.gh and durable. They are suitable for offices   40
>res, supermarkets and public reception places.   50

```
.    2    3    4    5    6    7    8    9    10
```

desired, a very heavy-duty super-tough tile is   10
;o available which can stand up to the heaviest   20
.r. These are ideal for hypermarkets; they can   30
:hstand wear from heavily-loaded trolleys. The   40
;e and speed with which they can be cleaned has   50
be seen to be believed. Visit our showroom to   60
.mine the excellent range of colours available.   70

```
.    2    3    4    5    6    7    8    9    10
```

Chapter 33

File Copies

It is always a good idea to keep a copy in your files of any letter or other document you send in connection with goods you order, complaints you make, agreements for work to be carried out, etc. If at some later stage you encounter any problems, you can refer back to the exact date on which the correspondence was sent and the precise words you used.

The file copy may be made while the original is being typed or printed by taking a carbon copy. Alternatively, if you use a computer you can print out a second copy. If you have access to a photocopier you may even take a photocopy to use as your file copy.

33.1 Guidelines

Taking a carbon copy

A carbon copy can be made on any typewriter, or on a printer which is able to feed single sheets rather than using continuous computer paper.

1 Place a sheet of plain paper on the table.

2 Place a sheet of carbon paper on top of this, with the carbon impregnated surface facing downwards.

3 Place your 'top sheet' of paper on top; if you use a sheet with a printed heading, the printing should be facing upwards.

4 Pick up the set of sheets so that the bottom sheet is facing you and the top sheet facing away from you, and insert them into the typewriter.

5   When the set of papers is positioned ready for typing, the carbon impregnated side of the carbon paper should be facing away from you.

If desired, four or five file copies can be produced in this way, simply by increasing the number of carbon papers and copy sheets. The clarity of the file copy decreases with an increase in the number of sheets of paper involved, though you may be able to increase the pressure if your typewriter has a pressure switch. Check your machine manual for instructions.

Correcting typing errors on carbon copies

1   Turn up one or two line spaces to bring the error to an accessible position.

2   Pull forward the top sheet and the carbon paper.

3   Apply a thin coating of paint-out fluid to the error and allow this to dry before replacing the carbon sheet and the top paper, otherwise the paint-out fluid will spoil your carbon paper.

4   Replace the carbon paper and top sheet and return the page to the correct line of type ready for typing in the correct letter(s).

5   After painting out the error on the top sheet, type in the correct letter(s).

33.2 Exercise

Read the guidelines before attempting this exercise. Take one file copy using carbon paper (or print a second copy if you are using a computer). Write 'File Copy' in the top right hand corner of the copy to identify it clearly.

As an alternative to centring the 'home' address, it may be typed across the page with extra spaces between the items so that it extends from margin to margin. Some people like to include their name, as shown on the exercise. You may also turn up one line space and use the underscore key to type a line from margin to margin.

Cheryl S Jowett   24 Skell Road   Preston   Lancashire   PR2 2LX

Today's date

Mr F Boucher
Service Manager
Mantype Supplies Ltd
Montague Lane
Southport
Merseyside
PR9 3JE

Dear Mr Boucher

MANTYPE 621 MANUAL TYPEWRITER

I am in receipt of your Invoice Number S/65001/B for £109.54.
The invoice lists a number of items such as service to a disk
drive and replacement of a connection cable.

My typewriter was serviced by you a few weeks ago, but my machine
is a Mantype 621 manual typewriter, which has no electrical
components - and it certainly does not have a disk drive.

It would appear that the Invoice sent to me was intended for
another customer, and I should be obliged if you would check your
records. A copy of Invoice Number S/65001/B is enclosed. I have
not yet received an invoice for the service and repairs to my
typewriter.

Yours sincerely

C S Jowett (Miss)

Enc

33.3 Tips

Always make sure that your file copy is easily identifiable. Write the
letter 'F' or the words 'File Copy' in the top right hand corner of the
page. Some people use coloured paper for file copies. A coding system
may be used for copies; yellow paper may be used for copies of
correspondence, for example, blue for reports, etc.

People using a computer may not wish to retain a 'hard copy' of the document in a file. They may prefer to retain it 'on file' on the floppy disk.

33.4 Proof-reading

The following passage contains some typographical errors. Proof-read the passage and see if you can identify all the errors. Your proof-reading skills may be checked against the key on p. 199.

When you have finished proof-reading, type a correct version of the passage, taking a file copy.


```
                F I L E     C O P I E S

In an ofice a typist is expected to make a file
copy ofall business letters,   memos and most other
documents  with out  being  instructed  to  do  so.
to do so.   However, an instruction will usually be
be given if several copies is requireed.    This
request may be given in varous ways, for example:

(a)    3 carbon copies please.

(b    1 + 3 copies.    (This means 1 top copy plus
      3 file copies(

A request for '3 copies' could be confusing.   Does
it mean the original plus 2 carbon copies,   or Does
it mean 3 carbon copies?.   Of course the typist can
alwyas clarify the request,   but the author may not
be available for discussion and time may be wasted.

      If in doubt,   the typist should produce the
highest number of file copies.    It is useful too
establish a mutually acceptable arrangement between
typits  and  authors  to  adopt  one  of  the  methods
suggested above
```

33.5 Speed Development

Wor

Additional copies of documents are often taken in
a business organisation and sent to other members
of staff in order to keep them informed about any
particular matter. A list of the people who have
received a copy is usually typed on the file copy
for reference purposes. This is called a distribution list, or alternatively a circulation list.

1   2   3   4   5   6   7   8   9   10

Where a single copy of a document is sent to each
person the term distribution list is appropriate.
The words 'copy to' or the letters 'cc' generally
precede the list of names. Where one copy of the
document is passed around to all the named people
the term circulation list is applicable. Each of
the people on the list writes his signature close
to his name to show that he has seen (and perhaps
even read) the document, before passing it to one
of the other individuals on the circulation list.

1   2   3   4   5   6   7   8   9   10

Chapter 34

Setting Information Out in Table Form

Tabulation facilities are provided on all but the most basic portable typewriters. The typist may set tabulator stops at any point across the page. By pressing the tabulator (tab) key (See Fig. 29 p. 128) the typing point is moved automatically to the pre-set positions. Some typewriters have tab stops set at five-space intervals across the carriage, and it is obviously fairly inconvenient if these stops cannot be changed. Most typewriters allow the typist to set tab stops at any desired position. The majority of word processing programs have tab stops pre-set at 'default' positions, but these can be changed as desired.

The use of tab stops is most helpful when typing columns of information, either words or figures. Check your user manual for instructions on setting and clearing tab stops.

Various types of tab stop are available on electronic typewriters and word processing programs: *left aligned, right aligned* (or flush right), *decimal* and *centred*. Check your user manual to see how many of these different tab settings are available on your machine, and for instructions on how to use them. A left aligned tab is generally used for information (or data) in the form of words, but there are occasions when you might want to use a centred or right aligned tab for text items. Whole numbers may be left or right aligned, depending on whether they are figures to be totalled; where totals are involved, the figures are usually right aligned. Decimal numbers are aligned on the decimal point, and a decimal tab is useful for this purpose.

34.1 Guidelines

Setting out the table

The process of setting out a table involving columns of words and/or figures is known as 'tabulation'. A simple table involving four columns

167

of data is shown here. Follow the instructions below to type the table, and this will help you to establish a routine for typing almost any table.

```
Multi-Modem    Without Autodial    Code 7796    £595
Multi-Modem    With Autodial       Code 7799    £654
Modem-Boost    Single Channel      Code 8844    £425
Modem-Boost    Double Channel      Code 8855    £550
```

11 + ④ + 16 + ④ + 9 + ④+ 4 = 52 ÷ 2 = 26

1 **Decide on column spaces**   Before starting work, decide on the number of spaces you intend to leave between the columns for the 'column space'. For this table leave four spaces between the columns, as indicated by the figures in circles on the example above.

2 **Clear tab stops**   All previously set tab stops must be cleared.

3 **Find the column width**   Count the width (in letter spaces) of the *widest item* of data in each column, and make a note of these below the columns, as shown on the example above.

4 **Find the centre point**   Move the typing point (or the cursor) to the centre point of the paper. (See p. 127 to remind you of the method, but *do not* set a tab at this point).

5 **Find the left margin**   Find the total of the numbers for each column and each column space; divide by two and make a note of this number. Backspace this number of spaces from the centre point (e.g. in the example shown above you will backspace 26 times).

6 **Set the left margin**   Set the left margin at this point.

7 **Set the tab stops**   From the left margin position, press the space bar (or move the cursor) once for each number in the width of the first column *and* the first column space (e.g. in the example press the space bar 11 times plus 4 times for the column space). Set the first tab stop at this position.

   Press the space bar (or move the cursor) once for each number in the next column and column space (e.g. in the example press the space bar 16 times plus 4 times for the column space). Set the second tab stop at this position.

   Press the space bar/cursor once for each number in the next column and column space (e.g. 9 + 4) and set the third tab stop at this position.

8 **Right margin**   There is no need to set a right margin for this type of work. However, if you wish to do so, press the space bar/cursor once for each number in the final column. Set the right margin at this point.

9 **Typing the table**   Type the first item at the left margin. Press the tab key to move to the first tab stop postion. Type the second item. Press the tab key to move to the second tab stop position and type the third item. Press the tab key to move to the third tab stop position and type the final item of the table shown in the example. Then press the return key and type the remaining lines of the table in the same way.

34.2 Exercises

Follow the general procedure described in the guidelines. Use left aligned (or 'normal') tab stops. Note that the tables have not been set out correctly in the exercises—when you type them, ensure that the spaces between the columns are equal in each table. Type each table on a separate sheet.

   When you have typed one table, remember to clear the tab stops before setting the tabs for the next table.

Exercise 1

W R Fortune	S B Taberer	A Adamson	L Gray
K Jones	K Ewens	O Wilson	K Down
S J Okimani	C Davies	F Gleight	B Low
L Al-Layho	M Pushka	G Simms	R Kay

Exercise 2

A C Parmenter	44	R Williams	45	L Vincent	32
M Springbett	37	E Scibetta	35	T Fox	49
Z O Friedberger	29	I Mauchant	47	M Vannozzi	33

Exercise 3

Microdisk Library Case	210 x 150 x 38 mm	£5.⁹
Minidisk Library Case	159 x 159 x 40 mm	£6.⁵
Diskette Library Case	240 x 228 x 45 mm	£8.²
Minifloppy Manager Box	171 x 165 x 40 mm	£8.⁷
Floppy Manager Box	241 x 229 x 44 mm	£9.⁵

Exercise 4

997	442	376	221	449	307	41	517
122	447	309	64	645	551	992	76
331	922	417	559	870	203	450	772
995	98	332	87	775	317	789	200
55	288	397	606	743	310	100	94

34.3 Tips

Always remember to clear all existing tab stops before starting to set out a new table.

Bear in mind that the longest line in a column may not be the first line; check through each column of the table to ensure that you find the longest line.

Do not leave too many spaces between columns. Depending on the number of columns and the amount of information in each column, you can leave anything from two to eight letter spaces. Four letter spaces is a useful column width for the majority of the work you do. Always use equal column spacing on each table.

If you use a computer, remember that it is necessary to press the return key at the end of each line of the table. The wraparound function is not appropriate for this type of work.

34.4 Proof-reading

The following passage has been printed twice. The first copy has been typed correctly, but the second copy contains typographical errors.

Proof-read the second passage and see if you can identify all the errors.
Your proof-reading skills may be checked against the key on p. 200.
    When you have finished proof-reading, type the first passage to gain
additional practice in setting out tables.

ELECTRONIC PRODUCTS EXHIBITION

You are invited to visit the Electronic Products
Exhibition at the Cranbourne Centre in Bristol.
You will see thousands of new products and have the
opportunity to attend practical workshop demon-
strations with in-depth technical information.

Sunday	18 May	11.00 am to 4.30 pm
Monday	19 May	10.00 am to 6.30 pm
Tuesday	20 May	10.00 am to 8.30 pm
Wednesday	21 May	10.00 am to 4.00 pm

Do not lose this ticket - it will allow you FREE
entry to the Exhibition. Entry without this ticket
will cost £3.50.

ELECTRONIC PRODUCTS EXHIBITION

You are invited to visit the Electronic Products
exhibition at the Cranborne Centre in Bristol. You
will see hundreds of new products and will have the
opportunity of attending practical workshop demons-
strations with in - depth technical information.

Sunday	18 May	11.00 am to 5.30 pm
Monday	18 May	10.00 am to 6.30 pm
tuesday	20 May	10.00 pm to 8.30 pm
Wenesday	21 May	10.00 am to 4 00 pm

Do not loose this ticket - it will allow you free
entry to the Exhibition. Entry without this
ticket will cost 3.50.

34.5 Speed Development

Wor

Consideration should always be given to using the   1
most appropriate type of paper for a document. A   2
well-displayed document looks much better on good   3
quality paper. The two major types of paper used   4
for typed documents are called 'bond' and 'bank'.   5
Bank paper is fairly flimsy and it is mainly used   6
for carbon copies; bond is used for the top copy.   7

    1   2   3   4   5   6   7   8   9   10

The quality of a paper is indicated by its weight   1
and a ream packet of paper is usually marked with   2
70 gsm, 80 gsm, 90 gsm and so on. The higher the   3
number, the better is the quality. The abbrevia-   4
tion 'gsm' stands for grams per square metre. It   5
is usual to type most business documents on 80 or   6
90 gsm bond paper. One ream contains 500 sheets.   7

    1   2   3   4   5   6   7   8   9   10

Chapter 35

Decimal Alignment and Right Alignment of Columns

In columns containing figures with a decimal point, the decimal point should be aligned (i.e. one below the other). This is known as decimal alignment. Where there are only two places of decimals, as with amounts of money, this obviously also results in right alignment. However, as shown in the example below, it is possible to align figures on the decimal point when the numbers contain varying numbers of decimal places.

Right alignment may be carried out on columns containing either figures or text, as shown in the example below.

DECIMAL ALIGNMENT		RIGHT ALIGNMENT	
		Figures	Text
£125.56	234.756	131,220	Disks
£74.96	4.5	25,763	Ribbons
£331.00	12.45	4,904	Pens
£5.33	152.002	882	Staplers

35.1 Guidelines

Manual typewriter

For either decimal alignment or right alignment of columns, set the tab stop(s) for the longest line in each column, as described in the last chapter. When typing the table, move to the tab stop position for any decimal or right aligned column. The longest line of figures is started at this point. Use the space bar to move along to the appropriate starting point for other figures in the column, so that when the number is typed the decimal point will be aligned, or all figures (or text) will end at the same point.

Electronic typewriters and computers

The way in which automatic decimal aligned and right aligned tab stops operate varies from machine to machine. The decimal aligned tab stop is, on many machines, set *at* the decimal point position; when the figures are typed, the figures are automatically 'backspaced' to the correct position.

The right aligned tab stop is usually set at the last letter position of a column; when the figures are typed they are automatically 'backspaced' to the correct position.

Check with your user manual for instructions on setting and using right aligned and decimal aligned tab stops. If you type a table with column headings, you will have to set two 'ruler lines' on your word processing program, one with left aligned tabs for the column headings, and one with decimal and/or right aligned tabs for the columns.

It takes a little practice to ensure that you are setting the decimal and right aligned tab stops in the correct position when 'setting up' a table. Until you gain more experience with both keyboarding and with your electronic typewriter or word processing program, you may wish to follow the simple procedure described above for manual typewriters.

35.2 Exercises

Read the information in the guidelines and the tips section before attempting these exercises. Note that the column headings are aligned with the start of the longest item in the column. Leave a clear line space after a column heading and before the total line for effective communication of the information contained in the tables.

Exercise 1

Type the following table, using decimal alignment.

	NORMAL	SALE	SAVING
Flight	£739.39	£550.10	£189.29
Accommodation	£375.25	£240.65	£134.60
Insurance	£12.80	£9.95	£2.85
TOTAL	£1,127.44	£800.60	£326.74

Exercise 2

Type the following table, using decimal alignment.

	YEAR 1	YEAR 2
Trade	£16,003.37	£11,507.45
Holiday Pay	£1,241.03	£908.66
Value Added Tax	£859.44	£596.91
Rental	£1,456.95	£889.04
Other Taxation	£994.66	£706.95
Other Charges	£1,388.65	£1,004.33
TOTAL	£21,944.10	£15,613.34

Exercise 3

Type the following table. Use left alignment for the second column and right alignment for the third column.

DISKMAN MAINTENANCE CONTRACTS

Diskman Service Group will maintain your Diskman computers at very reasonable contract prices. The contract, which allows for up to four visits in one year, includes all labour but excludes parts.

Model DO/1150	125 K	£99.50
Model DA/2205	256 K	£250.00
Model DD/3142	20 Mb	£575.00
Model DD/5366	80 Mb	£1,100.00
Model DW/6971	300 Mb	£1,450.00
Model DD/9562	300 Mb	£1,600.00

Exercise 4

Type the following staff list. Use right alignment for the second column.

```
     'FLEXETTE' LIMITED - GENERAL OFFICE STAFF


     Mr E F Schwarz              Office Manager
     Mr G Cranmer-Crick            Chief Clerk
     Ms S E Hines                   Supervisor
     Mrs B Nehemiah                      Clerk
     Ms T Smollett                   Secretary
     Miss R Burns               Audio-Typist
```

35.3 Tips

Headings may be added to columns of figures or words in tables. As with other headings, you may use capitalisation, underlining and emboldening for emphasis. Leave one clear line space after a column heading to separate it from the table.

When setting up your table and counting the longest line in each column, bear in mind that the longest line may, in some cases, be the heading to the column.

If you use a computer to type tables with totals, your word processing program may have a useful 'add' function that allows you to add columns or rows of figures. Check your system manual to see if this function is available on your program.

35.4 Proof-reading

The following table has been printed twice. The first copy has been typed correctly but there are typographical errors in the second copy. Proof-read the second passage and see if you can identify all the errors. Your proof-reading skills may be checked against the key on p. 200.

When you have finished proof-reading, type the first passage to gain additional practice in typing tables.

DEVVER TYPEWRITER DUST COVERS

Protect your machine with our new, top-quality anti-static typewriter dust covers. These smart designer-styled equipment covers are available in a wide range of bright colours.

MATERIAL	MACHINE	CODE	PRICE
Vinyl	Typerite 221	XL/003	£22.00
Vinyl	Typerite 201	L/001	£19.99
Vinyl	Mostype 003	S/100	£12.45
Nylon/PVC	Typerite 233	NXL/013	£31.40
Nylon/PVC	Truetype C	NL/011	£23.00
Nylon/PVC	Mostype 007	N/021	£19.75

AVAILABLE FROM YOUR LOCAL DEALER

DEVVER TYPWRITER DUSTY COVERS

Protest your machine with our new, top-quality anti-static equipment dust covers. These smart desinger-styled typewriter covers are available in a range of bright colours.

MATERIAL	MACHINE	CODE	PRICES
Vinyl	Typerite 221	XL/013	£22.00
Vynil	Typerite 201	L/001	£19.99
Vinyl	Mostype 003	S/100	£12.45
Nylon/PVC	Typerite 233	NXL/013	£31.44
Nylon/PVC	Truetype C	NL/011	£23.00
Nylon/PVC	Mostyper 007	N/021	£19 75

AVAILABLE NOW FROM YOUR LOCAL DEALER

35.5 Speed Development

Wor

We all know that electricity is dangerous, but do   1
you know that a human being can be killed by less   2
current than it takes to blow a fuse? For safety   3
in the computer room all the electrical equipment   4
should either be fitted with a power breaker plug   5
or an ordinary plug should be fitted into a power   6
breaker socket. The power breaker offers protec-   7
tion by detecting the smallest leak of current to   8
earth; within 30 milliseconds of sensing the leak   9
it cuts off all power to an electrical appliance.   1C

    1   2   3   4   5   6   7   8   9   10

Chapter 36

Review and Revision

This section is useful for reinforcing key reaches and for improving accuracy. Use a line length of 55. Do not type all the exercises at one sitting. Use the chapter as a revision aid, spending short periods of concentrated practice on any aspect you feel needs review and consolidation.

36.1 Key Reach Review

Home Key Row

```
asdfgfa ;lkjhj; asdfgfa ;lkjhj; asdfgfa; ;lkjhj;a
fgfdsa jhjkl; fgfdsa jhjkl; fdsa jkl; gfdsa hjkl;
```

Home Key Row and Third Row

```
frf juj ded kik sws lol aqa ;p; ftf jyj fgf; jhja
qap; wsol edik rfuj tfyj gftf hjyj edik wsol q;ap
```

Home Key Row and First Row

```
fvf jmj dcd k,k sxs l.l aza ;a; fbf jnj fgfa jhj;
za;a xs.l cd,k vfmj bfnj za;a xs.l cd,k vfmj bfnj
```

All Alphabet Letters

```
;p;p; aqaza lol.l swsxs kik,k dedcd jujmj; frfvf;
jyjnj ftfbf fgfga jhjh; ;p;p; aqaza lol.l; swsxs;

abc def ghi jkl mno pqr stu vwx yz.
zyx wvu tsr qpo nml kji hgf edc ba.
```

Figure Row

```
12345 09876 54321 67890 123454 098767 54321 67890
1029 3847 5610 2938 5467 3289 2190 4321 7890 4576
```

179

36.2 Individual Letter Practice

If you have difficulty with a particular letter, use the appropriate lines from the list below for revisionary practice.

A   Ask at this address about all our acoustic hoods
Attach an automatic arm at the back of that gate
I accessed all that data in the accounts package

B   Bert learnt about bits, bytes, buffers and Basic
The batch in the big black box was bought by Bob
Bring the big bag to the bank on Bibby Boulevard

C   Check the circuit calculations on the calculator
Chris cancelled the computer security conference
Chip and Company created a complete circuit card

D   Discuss delivery dates for disk drives and desks
The directory, or index, describes all documents
Dan Deed used a dedicated key to delete the data

E   Every effort is needed to meet the delivery date
Read the error message then exit from the system
The electronic editor is effective and efficient

F   Fetch the file of frequency figures for the firm
Frank fitted five flexible deflectors for effect
Format fifty floppy disks for the safety officer

G   Get the grey gauge graded and give it to Gregory
Gather the genuine goods together, and get going
Give us a guide to using these graphics packages

H   Hugh Hershel helped Harry to handle the hardware
Teach Heather the method for checking this batch
The machine has a heater and a heavy hinged hood

I   If the index is right, it gives this information
Miss Ibis is included in the identification list
I intend to input the sixty invoices immediately

J John J Jackson joined the Jersey Journal in July.
  The ink jet injector jammed and just injured Jay.
  Major Jarret just enjoys his job as a journalist.

K Check the bank of black keys on the keyboard kit.
  Ask Kate and Ken to keep a look out for the disk.
  I know how to take the back block off the linker.

L Leave the pallet labels on this low level loader.
  Lillian always likes to log off by eleven lately.
  Recall all the faulty old visual displays please.

M Make the maintenance man mend the master machine.
  Mr Mims must remember to mark the magnetic media.
  We import micros, minis and mainframe computers.

N Disconnect the nodes on the new internal network.
  Note that no numerical analysis is necessary now.
  Ben can run this new communications centre alone.

O Your operator opened the output folders too soon.
  In our opinion, you omitted the original opening.
  Your order for our goods does not quote our code.

P Philip prepared the page and printed it promptly.
  This page is important, so proofread it properly.
  Please prepare simple passwords for these people.

Q Quote our price for quite high quality equipment.
  They required a cheque quickly for that quantity.
  A quick question; what is our quota this quarter?

R Read the error prompts and respond appropriately.
  Mr Rose refused to report our request for a rise.
  Our representative, Roger Reardon, arrived early.

S Sam scrolls the screen display from side to side.
  We must use secret passwords for system security.
  She sent several single sided disks to the staff.

T The typist transmitted the typed text by teletex.
  Theresa tried to test the terminal last Thursday.
  Tim operated the telex terminal without training.

U   Unfortunately our users are uncertain about this
    You must undertake the use of the utilities file
    Unless they understand, faults may go undetected

V   Vivian interviewed every van driver this evening
    Videotex proved very valuable for their visitors
    Vanda and Neville have evaluated this video unit

W   We wondered whether you would write on Wednesday
    We want to know how, when, why and where it went
    We knew the workers would want new work-stations

X   Tex expected the extra text to be extracted next
    The experts fixed these sixty extra export boxes
    The text index showed a maximum of six documents

Y   You may make a study of my yearly file every day
    Mary and Harry were sorry about the poor quality
    You said that you paid for it yourself yesterday

Z   Lizzie was amazed at the size of the sales zones
    Buy Zachary four dozen of the buzzers, size zero
    The copier zooms to all sizes, from zero to nine

36.3 Alphabet Review Sentence Practice

Each of these short paragraphs contains all the letters of the alphabet. They provide excellent practice material for improving your accuracy. If you have difficulty with any particular letter of the alphabet, revise the key reach with the appropriate key reach review (36.1) and individual letter practice (36.2).

Costs for training courses vary considerably, and you will not be amazed to find that those provided by commercial firms are quite a bit more expensive than those offered by further education colleges, which are likely to be just as good.

This is a new word processing package of excellent quality. It has something called WYSIWYG (pronounced 'wizziwig'), which stands for 'what you see is what you get'. In other words the screen lets you view the text just as it will be printed out.

When you start to learn about word processors and computers, you feel there are dozens of jargon terms. It makes everything extremely difficult to understand at first, but you very quickly get to know the meanings of the technical terms.

We sell floppy disks in three sizes and lockable disk storage boxes. Ribbons and printwheels are available in more than a dozen different typestyles. Why not buy a trolley for your visual display unit? Just telephone our enquiries office for advice.

You can order by post or by telephone, but if you prefer it we can accept your order by telex or by fax. Our sales staff enjoy fulfilling your orders quickly. If you want to make the trip to our depot, just give us a 'buzz' on the phone before you come.

The term 'zap' used on some systems means that a
section of text will be cut out and deleted. The
terms 'quit' or 'exit' are used on several word
processing packages when a document is to be filed.
The operations are the same - it's just that the
terms used in word processing are not standardised.

Dot matrix printers have a vertical column of needle
which strike through the ribbon to mark the letters
on the paper. Ink jet printers spray the letters
onto the paper, and no ribbon is required. Daisy-
wheel printers have a round printing wheel embossed
with letters of the appropriate size at the end of
each 'daisy' petal.

Because of the risk of unauthorised entry to areas o
the complex where security is essential, we have jus
decided to install an access control system. Every
member of staff will be required to tap out his/her
personal key code to gain access to various zones.

The new range of executive shredders, available in a
range of sizes, are fully automatic. They combine
flexibility with mechanical robustness. The
cross-cutting techniques reduce your documents to
extremely small pieces, and they make short work of
staples or paperclips without injury to the blades.

Answers

Test Your Knowledge

Chapter 1

1 Because all operations are carried out manually.
2 Keyboard; platen; carriage; print mechanism.
3 Central processing unit.
4 Input device or keyboard; VDU; external memory storage system (or disk drive); printer.

Chapter 2

1 It reduces the effect of direct light onto the VDU screen, enabling text to be read more easily. It is also said to reduce the emission of the electrostatic field from the VDU screen.
2 Opening doors and windows; extractor fan; air-conditioning; electronic air cleaner (ioniser).
3 By housing the printer in an acoustic hood.
4 The arms should rise slightly from the elbow to bring the forearms parallel to the slope of the keys of the keyboard. The elbows should take a restful position close to the body.

Chapter 3

1 It protects the platen and thereby increases its life.
2 Single sheet at a time—manually; single sheet at a time—automatically; automatic feed of continuous stationery.
3 The process by which an operator prepares the computer for use. This may necessitate the loading of a program into the memory of the computer. On some computers it may also be necessary to go through a security clearance procedure involving the use of passwords to allow the user access to data stored in the memory.

Chapter 4

1   The word *font* refers to the style or shape of the print.
2   Points or pitch.
3   1; 1.5 (or 1½); 2.
4   In standard spacing each letter or figure takes up the same amount of space on a line. Proportional spacing is a method of allocating space proportional to the size of the letter or figure being typed, e.g. **i** takes up less space on the line than **w**.

Chapter 5

1   Proof-reading is the process of checking a typed page, text on a VDU screen or a printed hard copy, for accuracy and completeness.
2   Correctness; completeness; comparison; co-operation.
3   Paint-out fluid; correction paper; correction ribbon.
4   (a) Insert a space
    (b) Begin a new paragraph here
    (c) Let the original wording stand.

Chapter 6

1   Because the first six keys on the top row of letters at the left hand side of the keyboard read QWERTY.
2   (a) There are two shift keys (and one shift lock)
    (b) The shift keys are situated one to the left and one to the right of the bottom row of keys, near the space bar.
3   Your answer may include any or all of the following:
    (a) The QWERTY keys
    (b) The number row of keys
    (c) The symbol keys
    (d) A numeric key pad
    (e) Additional function keys
    (f) User defined or programmable keys
    (g) Cursor movement keys.

Chapter 7

1   asdfghjkl;
2   They are the guide keys from which the fingers move out to depress other keys on the keyboard, and to which the fingers must return 'home' as soon as another key has been pressed.
3   The typing action for a manual typewriter is firm, sharp and precise. The action for an electronic typewriter is light but precise.

Proof-reading Keys

Key to Chapter 5

Dry Transfer Lettering

We can all probably remember as children, getting
coloured transfers which we moistened and placed on
a hand or arm, pretending they where tattoos.
These these are known as wet transfers and they
were also used commercially in graphics design. A
graphics designer, dai Davies, developed adry
letter transfer which was marketed in 1926.
It has changed the world of graphics design.
Anyone now can insert professional looking letters
on diagrams and posters by simply rubbing a sheet
to deposite the letter on paper The number of
fonts and points available is almost endless.

Key to Chapter 8

When you learn to use a keyboard you are training
your fingers to to move away from the home keys in
a particular direction, and for given distance.
it is therefore important to return each finger to
its home key immediately after moving to strike
another key so that the the next 'Key reach' will
be accurate.

Key to Chapter 9

In the early stages of keyboard training you should
not (should not) attempt to correct any errors you
may make. You main aim at this stage is to learn
the correct key reaches. If the key reach is
accurate then the printed text will be accurate.
If you have struck the wrong key by mistake, (then)
correcting the error on the page (or on the screen
is of little benefit. Direct your practise to
learning () correct key reaches so that you strike
the correct key with (with) the appropriate finger.

Key to Chapter 10

Many people insist that 'touch typists should be
able to type page after page of text without ever
looking at the keyboard Inexperienced typists
therefore feel a sense of guilt if they steal a
glance now and (then) at the keyboard to gain
confidence. Obviously it is inefficient to look at
the keyboard all the time, but research has shown
that even the most experience typists are
constantly glancing at the keyboard in much the
same (the same) way that a driver is constantly
glancing in the mirror without taking his attention
from the road.

Key to Chapter 11

When you are using a word processor, the
wordwrap facility takes care of line
endings automatically, and there is no
(no) need for the operator to use the return
key when typing continous paragraphs of
text. However, it is necessary to use
the return to insert a 'hard return'
at the end of (;) a heading, a paragraph, a
single line of text, each line of a (of a)
tabulated statement and whenever an extra
line space is required.

Key to Chapter 12

If you use a wordprocessor, it is in your
own interests to take care of your floppy
disks. Keep them away from sources of heat
(heat such as radiators or sunny window
sills), and from sources of magnetic
radiation (such as the System itself or
even the telephone). When not in use
disks should be stored in a rigid case.

Key to Chapter 13

You should have developed the habit by now
of proofreading your work. If you have made
errors, try to identify the causes of these
these errors. In many cases they will be
caused by incorrect key reaches. Practice
the faulty key reaches looking at your
fingers to ensure that your hand movements
are correct and the reach confidently made

Key to Chapter 14

Listing Paper

a computer programme is written and then put
into the computer What has been input can
be printed had this printed from is known as
a program listing. The program listing
because it is usually very long, is printed
on continuous stationary which has bands of
of fine lines and open spaces evenly
distributed throughout the length of the paper
This has led to this type of continuus
stationery being termed listing paper.

Key to Chapter 15

The type face of manual typewriters, golf ball type
elements and printwheels becomes 'dirty' through a
build up of ink from continuosly strikeing the rpin
ribbon If this is allowed to accumilate the
centre of leters such as a, p, b and e become
blocked. It is good practice to clean the typeface
at regular intevals using the appropriate method.

Key to Chapter 16

Officer Security

Computers can offer great flexability in the
preparation of documents. They may be edited a
number of times quiet easily. However, some
doucments may be private and confidencail and what
happens to the the descarded drafts of the document
could be vitaly important to the busisness. For
this reason many businesses use paper shredders in
in the office. All unwanted paperwrok which would
normally go into a waste paper baskit, is put
thorugh the shredder.

Key to Chapter 17

Fire Precuations

Wherever their is electricity and electrical
equipment in use there is the potential danger off
fire resulting from an electrical fautl For this
reason evry home and buisness should have a fire
extinguisher Special extinguishers which do not
conduct electricity must be used. Thede
containining bromochlordiflourmethane are said to
be efficient fighting fires caused through
electrical faults

Key to Chapter 18

Envelops Galore

Everyone needs envelopes at some time, weather for
the home, Sports Club, educatoinal edstablishment
of business. We have the right envelop for each
ocasion, from perfumed for the romantic, to self-
adhesive for the overworked.
Why not advertise your business by having your
Company Logo and addresss printed on the envelope.
Send for detials of our range of envelopes today.

Key to Chapter 19

SEARCH OR REPLACE

The search and replace facility offered by most
computers is extremely useful. If a particularly
word is spelt incorrectly through out a document,
you can instruct the system to find all instances
of the word and to replace them with the correct
spelling. alternatively, you may wish to replace
word such as 'automobile' with the word 'car'
throughout the document, to or replace an
an abbreviation such as vdu with the full word.

Key to Chapter 20

Copys of Documents

The traditional way of obtaining additional copies
of a document is to make copies at the time of
typing the orginal. This could be very time
consuming, dependnig on the accuracy of the typist
because typing errors have be to corrected on
on each carbon copy. In many organisations carbon
copies are not longer used, and copies are now
made on the photo-copier.

Key to Chapter 21

Printer Transfer Switch

Computer printers can be expensive, especially when
adcoustic hoods must be be bought to reduce noise.
However, printer use is intermittent most of the
Typist's time being taken up with inputting data
into the computer. Costs canbe reduced if two
typists share the same printer by use of a printer
printer transfere switch.

Key to Chapter 22

Disk Care

Computer diskettes can pick up dust anddirt just li
anything else in your office. Tiny particals of di
on a diskette can result in scraches on the surface
which results in loss of dates. Magnetic feilds
found near your computer or telephone or other
electrical equipment can corrupt data stored on a
on a disk. Always store disks in the special
storeage boxes available from office equipment
companies.

Key to Chapter 23

Storage and Security

Paper storeage is always a problem in an office. As the amount and size of the storage cabinets have to be increased, with the consequent problem of where to sight the storage cabinets.

Computers are said to offer the the opportunity to elimanate the paper storage problem by dispensing with paper copies and storing all file data on disk, but this poses the problem of security. It's difficult for any one to remove a whole filing cabinet along with its files, but a disk or even a box of disks, is easily stolen or misled.

Key to Chapter 24

Trimplex Micro Systems have launched the TXM 576 microcomputer, a stand alone microcomputer based on an Intel 8086 processor and also incorpororating 640 Kbytes of host resident Ram. It also features 10 Mbytes of winchester disk storeage, and a single 360 Kbyte double sided, double dynasty floppy disk drive. The 4 inch colour monitor is adjustable for tilt, swivel and slides. For further details telephone 552 397961 or write to Tony Skear, Department 927, Trimplex MicroSystems, 72 South Vincent Street, Glasgow, G4 3PQ.

Key to Chapter 25

471.55 588 96 696 70 339.84 102.73 963 32 493.11

393 39 568.10 302 01 112.83 884.7 239.06 667 66

32 0 49 50 03 600.02 112.83 908.67 330.15 667.66

Key to Chapter 26

MoSta* Computer Desk

The MoSta Computer Desk offers you the vertasile workstation you have been waiting for. Here are just a few of its features: large enough to hold your computer and its perpherals; easy-moving MoGlide* castor; unique MoFeed* paper rake. Only –£250 each + Vat ($360 in USA). The following quality discounts apply (UK purchases only: 2 desks 5%, 5 desks 10%, 10 desks and over 15%.

* Registered Trade Mark of Mosley-Steele Ltd.

Key to Chapter 27

W A V E R L Y   S Y S T E M S

YOUR COMPANY SERVICE INCLUDES

Lease Contracts
Lease Rental and Hire-Purchase
Customer Data Base Systems
Maintainance and Service Contracts
Installation contracts
Net-work Systems and Multi User Systems

DEMONSTRATION AND SECOND-HAND MACHINES AVAILAIBLE

Key to Chapter 28

COMPUTERS IN HOTELS

The large hotel groups have been useing computers for some years. Owner's of many of the country's smaller hottels have now realised that a computer can improve efficiency in there establishment. Interest has now increased to such a level that computer exhibitions are devoted to the needs of the hotel industry. Softwear is available for all aspects of the trade including the following:

Advance Reservations

Depp.sits
Booking Charts
Correspondnence

Arrivals and Departures

Geust Accounts
Daily Balancing
Customised Analysis

Guest History

Selective Search
mailshots
Repeat Bookingings

Key to Chapter 29

PARAGAPHING

Some people beleive that paragraphs should be no longer that 5 lines, but it is difficult to be to be to precise. Certainly, very long paragraphs are likley to deter the reader. Shortparagraphs of two or three lines long give emphas is, but the valve of this is lost if too many short paragraphs are used.

Never have the first line of a paragraph at the end of the page. If this is likely to happen, start the paragraph on a continuation sheet. It is is easier to read and understand if there are at least 3 lines of text at the end of a end of a page with the rest of the paragraph continued on a seperate sheet.

Key to Chapter 30

'FLEXETTE' DISK FILEING CABINETS

Do you know that it is now possible to buy special fileing cabinets especially for your floppy disks. We provide a range forall sizes of disks;

Catalogue Number FDF/21 for 8' disks
Catalogue Number FDF/40 for 5¾" disks
Catalogue Number FDF/95 for 3½" disks

Each cabinet holds up to 100 disks and has 100 dividers.   As a special promotional incentive we are offerring a 5% reduction on single orders and and 12½% on orders of 5 or more cabinets (whilst present stocks last only).   Send for a price list today?

Key to Chapter 31

W H I T E   S P A C E

The area of a page of text on which their is no

typing is known as 'white space'. The creation of

white space around a paragraph or section of text

helps to emphasise that paragraph or section so

that it stands out from the rest of the text.

White space can be created by increasing the mar-

gin sizes all round, and the line spacing between

items or paragraphs.

> Sections of text may also be indented (or
> inset five or more spaces from both the
> left and right margins to provide added
> emphasis and to give an effective layout.

The effect of white space may also be achieved by

varying the line spacing of the text. The main

portion of the text, for example, may be typed in

double line spacing, with sub-paragraphs typed in

single line spacing, as in this passage.

Key to Chapter 32

29TH June

Miss Julie A Martin
67 White Acre
Saughall Bridge
Birmingham
B32 3PY

Dear Miss Martin

'PERM-A-TYPE' TYPEWRITER RIBBONS

Thank you for your intrest in our new range of typewriter ribbons.
We produce three types of ribbon, each of which is suitable for your
'Bravenue' electronic typwiter.

The 'Everlasting' fabric ribbon, code PT/EL3, costs only £2.95, and
is suitable for the majority ofwork you are likely to produce.
However, when you wish to impress your correspondent you should use
use one of our plastic carbon film ribbons.   The single-strike
crabon ribbon, code PT/SS3, gives a sharp image and costs only £187
The multi-strike carbon ribbon, code PT/MS3, costs a little more at
$4.66, but it lasts much longer.

Prices quoted are per ribbon.   The mimimum order size is five
ribbons of any one type.   We enclose an order form for yuour
convenience.Please be sure to quote the code number wen ordering.

Yours Sincerley
CAPITAL PERIPHERAL SUPPLIES LTD

Marjory Scruby (Mrs)
Supplies Manager

Enc

Key to Chapter 33

F I L E   C O P I E S

In an ~~ofi~~ce a typist is expected to make a file
copy o~~fal~~l business letters, memos and most other
documents wit~~h ou~~t being instructed to do so.
~~to do so.~~ However, an instruction will usually be
~~be~~ given if several copies ~~is~~ requir~~ed~~. This
request may be given in va~~rou~~s ways, for example:

(a)   3 carbon copies please.

(~~b~~   1 + 3 copies.   (This means 1 top copy plus
       3 file copies~~(~~

A request for '3 copies' could be confusing. Does
it mean the original plus 2 carbon copies, or ~~Does~~
it mean 3 carbon copies?~~(~~ Of course the typist can
al~~wya~~ clarify the request, but the author may not
be available for discussion and time may be wasted.

       If in doubt, the typist should produce the
highest number of file copies. It is useful t~~oo~~
establish a mutually acceptable arrangement between
ty~~pits~~ and authors to adopt one of the methods
suggested above~~(~~

Key to Chapter 34

ELECTRONIC PRODUCTS EXHIBITION

You are invited to visit the Electronic Products
exhibition at the Cranborne Centre in Bristol. You
will see hundreds of new products and will have the
opportunity of attending practical workshop demons-
strations with in - depth technical information.

Sunday	18 May	11.00 am to 5.30 pm
Monday	18 May	10.00 am to 6.30 pm
tuesday	20 May	10.00 pm to 8.30 pm
Wenesday	21 May	10.00 am to 4.00 pm

Do not loose this ticket - it will allow you free
entry to the Exhibitition. Entry without this
ticket will cost 3.50.

Key to Chapter 35

DEVVER TYPWRITER DUSTY COVERS

Protest your machine with our new, top-quality
anti-static equipment dust covers. These
smart designer-styled typewriter covers are
available   in   a   range   of   bright   colours.

MATERIAL	MACHINE	CODE	PRICES
Vinyl	Typerite 221	XL/013	£22.00
Vynil	Typerite 201	L/001	£19.99
Vinyl	Mostype 003	S/100	£12.45
Nylon/PVC	Typerite 233	NXL/013	£31.44
Nylon/PVC	Truetype C	NL/011	£23.00
Nylon/PVC	Mostyper 007	N/021	£19.75

AVAILABLE NOW FROM YOUR LOCAL DEALER